Ron Santo: For Love of Ivy

The Autobiography of Ron Santo

Ron Santo
with
Randy Minkoff

Bonus Books, Inc., Chicago

©1993 by Bonus Books, Inc.

97   96   95   94   93   5   4   3   2

Library of Congress Catalog Card Number: 92–75928

International Standard Book Number: 0–929387–92–9

Bonus Books, Inc.
160 East Illinois Street
Chicago, Illinois 60611

Printed in the United States of America

To Ron, Jr., Jeff and Linda

Contents

Foreword

I was fortunate enough during my major league baseball career to play with and against some of the top athletes of any era. In my mind, Ron Santo was at the top of this list.

In many ways, Ron and I were a lot alike on the playing field. We came to play every day and wanted to win. We did whatever it took to get a triumph, even though we might not have had the best skills or tools in the world.

What set Ron Santo apart from so many other great ball players were three key ingredients: determination, excellence and dedication. Those three things best sum up Ron Santo the player, Ron Santo the individual.

Ron didn't have it easy. He had to overcome very difficult, adverse circumstances, dealing with playing with diabetes throughout his major league career. Many might not have ever been up to the task; Ron was.

No one I ever faced played the game harder than Ron Santo did. He was like that in every game he played for as a Chicago Cub, he was like that when he got out of the game and dove straight into the world of business and he is like that today as a Chicago Cubs' broadcaster. He always wanted to win and would do whatever it took to accomplish that goal.

The Big Red Machine of the 1970s would have had a very nice spot in their lineup for Ron Santo. We tried out many different people at third base and we were always seemingly looking for a "Ron Santo" type. If we had been lucky enough to obtain Ron Santo from the Cubs, I don't know how many more games we could have won.

He wasn't a flashy ballplayer, neither was I. He and I were taught the same things about playing the game: no splash, no glitz. You just got the job done. No high fives, no showboating, just giving it all you could each day.

I suppose Ron's achievements have always been overlooked by many because his Cubs' teams never made it to the playoffs or the World Series. It is a shame.

For no third baseman I ever played against or saw cross the white lines was better at his position. Check the numbers: they are Hall of Fame quality all the way. Mike Schmidt and Brooks Robinson, one future and one current Hall of Fame third baseman, had great talent. You have to mention Ron Santo at third base when you mention the greats, and he belongs right alongside the Schmidts and Robinsons. His numbers are right up there with the great ones. As a fielder, no one hustled more and covered as much ground as Ron Santo.

I know that some day, Ron will earn his proper spot in Cooperstown. We will finally be teammates. I know Ron Santo is a Hall of Fame individual and have no doubt that soon everyone else will realize he was a Hall of Fame baseball player.

It's a misconception that Ron had it easier playing in cozy Wrigley Field. What many fans—and the media—don't always understand is that Wrigley Field can often be a pitcher's ballpark when the wind howls in during April or May at the beginning of the year or September or October toward the end of the season. As many home runs as Ron got from the friendly winds were taken away from those not-so-friendly gusts.

I was fortunate enough to become friends with Ron during our playing days. That carried over to today. He, Ed Podolak, the former great Kansas City back, and myself played a lot of golf together. We are known as the three musketeers. On the golf course, Ron is the same type of quality competitor as he was as a player. He might not be as successful a golfer as he was a third baseman, but he tried just as hard.

Ron always believed that if you gave it your best, tried and put out 100 percent, you earned respect. Never mind if you lacked the talent or physical skills, Ron admired those who always did the best they could. It's an admirable quality.

He is the kind of individual you are proud to say is your friend. A friend for life. I'm proud to say Ron Santo is my friend.

Johnny Bench

Acknowledgements

The authors would like to thank the following people for their hours of assistance and support:

To Shari Lesser Wenk, our agent, who was an inspiration to the project and whose constant faith in the book kept things going. She is the best in the business.

To Ramona Race, whose computer genius helped keep the bugaboos from sidelining the work.

To the Cubs' public relations staff for helping to dig out the cobwebs and the boxscores.

To Thom and Wayne, for their support and encouragement to try two full-time jobs at the same time and not miss one major story; to Pac-Man and Kermit for keeping things on an even keel.

To Vicki, for her undying patience with long hours of phone calls and meetings to draw out the great stories.

To Gene and Enid Minkoff, for instilling the love of baseball in their son.

And to Sue Castorino Minkoff, who never lost faith in the writing side of her best friend, who volunteered numerous hours for rewriting and proofreading and who helped shepherd this book from its inception to its completion.

one

On the Air

I had made this drive so many times that I could have done it in my sleep. On this day in 1990, though, it was different.

Instead of driving along the shops and businesses on Addison Street toward Wrigley Field wondering about the pitcher I would be facing that day, I was thinking about what I was going to say on the air.

Nearly 15 years had passed since I retired from baseball, a game that I loved with a deep passion. For 15 years, I had made the drive through the narrow streets in Wrigleyville to my parking spot in the players' lot. I would put on a Chicago Cubs' uniform and go through a pregame regimen that would sometimes include taking a shot of insulin in the leg.

On this day, the drive was the same, but the thoughts were different. I was back at the park I love with the fans I love, but I wasn't wearing number 10: I was wearing a sweater and gloves on this cold, April day. And instead of being on the field, I was in the broadcast booth for the Chicago Cubs.

One thing was the same: the electricity in the ballpark on Opening Day is something that cannot be matched in any sport on any other day, as more than 37,000 fans wait for the first pitch that starts the annual odyssey toward what everyone prays will be October baseball.

Everyone is optimistic; everyone is eager. On this day, though, I was just a little bit more eager than anyone else.

As the teams warmed up, I was taken by surprise at the number of fans calling out to me; fifteen years is a long time to have been away. I had followed the Cubs religiously, but I hadn't spent much time at the ballpark. But they remembered. They remembered our 1969 club that still ranks as the most famous team in club history. Remembered the clicking of the heels after each win, the plays I made (and some I didn't make) at third base. The home runs. The base hits. My teammates.

Now I was facing a completely new challenge in the booth; if I slipped up on a statistic or made the wrong comment, the fans listening on the air wouldn't care if I was a Gold Glover at third or an All-Star for the National League.

I saw my new broadcast partners, Thom Brennaman, the son of the great Reds' broadcaster Marty Brennaman, and Bob Brenly, the longtime veteran catcher with the Giants, and they relaxed me. Thom, cool and professional, and Bob, gifted with a dry wit and keen insight to the game, spent hours with me during spring training helping me through the rough spots. At age 50, I was a rookie all over again. Only now it's not 1959 and it's not the Texas League. It's 1990 and it's the Cubs and the Philadelphia Phillies.

I had already done my pregame preparation, laying out

the notes and books I would refer to when it was my turn to add words of wisdom. I knew both Thom and Bob were probably nervous, too, but if they were, they weren't showing it.

The Cubs had asked us to throw out the ceremonial first pitch for Opening Day, which was a real honor. I had done it before during the playoffs, but this was something different, something special. The click of the cameras from the photographers is as clear as the sound of a bat.

But then we realized that immediately after the pitch, we had only precious moments to make the mad dash up through the stands to our perch in the broadcast booth. I guess I'm still in shape. I wasn't winded completely when we reached the WGN broadcast booth.

The cold winds off Lake Michigan have taken their unkind cuts at me as a hitter; how many times did I hit a ball that seemed destined for extra bases, only to have it blown in to some outfielder's waiting glove? On this Opening Day, the wind was howling again, and it was cold; the windows in our catbird's seat high atop the National League's oldest park were wide open so we could catch the sound and flavor on the air.

As Thom began his introduction of our new broadcast team, that famous Chicago wind knocked over the steaming cup of coffee I had placed right next to my papers and books.

"The Chicago Cubs are on the air!" was Brennaman's opening refrain.

"Goddammit!" was my first comment as a WGN broadcaster.

I quickly turned to Thom and saw the look of horror on his face; his eyes were bulging out, partly in disbelief, partly in shock. It wasn't exactly what I had in mind for my triumphant reunion with the Chicago Cubs.

My love affair with the Cubs had been born many years earlier in my hometown of Seattle, Washington. It was a relationship that would take me through my high school career, my two years in the minor leagues when I nearly walked out on the Cubs and major league baseball, through the depths of losing under the College of Coaches, through the rise of the team under fiery Leo Durocher, to my own day at Wrigley Field at the peak of my career and my sudden departure from the club to the arch-rival Chicago White Sox.

It was a relationship that had brought me tremendous joy and sadness, and now, sitting high above the most beautiful ballpark in the world, I couldn't help think of all the things that had happened in my life along the incredible journey that had brought me back here once again.

two

Sports Saved Me

I wasn't born with a third baseman's glove in my hand—they waited until I was two to get me started. I can't tell you what I went for in that first outing.

I do know that my father, for all the trouble he caused my family, did get me thinking about sports at a young age. I didn't know it at the time, but I was the second person in major league history to make it to the big leagues from Little League. Joey Jay was the first.

We all have dreams when we're kids; you stand at that plate and pretend you're hitting in Game Seven of the World Series with two outs in the ninth. But when you grow up in the 1940s in Seattle, Washington—before there was Major League baseball there—the most you can hope for is a shot at the Pacific Coast League. And we didn't have cable or Game of the Week, either.

When I was six, my father left home. We lived in an ethnic, middle class neighborhood called Garlic Gulch, and he was a bartender. He'd come home at 3:00 A.M., and you could cut the tension with a knife. He was a wonderful Italian man when he was sober, but, sadly, he had a drinking problem that made him vicious, which is how he was at 3:00 A.M. My mother, who was Swedish, would be furious, and they'd fight. I'd scramble out of bed to keep him from hitting her, but I was just a kid...and he would beat her.

They divorced when I was seven. My father had visitation rights to see me and my sister, Natalie, every two or three weeks. We'd wait for him on a corner, and he'd pick us up.

One day, he just didn't show up. I didn't see him again for twelve years.

I'm sure the lack of paternal guidance had an impact on my behavior, which wasn't always great. I got into a lot of trouble with a bunch of neighborhood kids, shooting out street lights with a BB gun, stealing cartons of cigarettes. I didn't even smoke, but at age 11, we had this club, and part of the initiation was to inhale. Well, the police caught us for the cigarette theft, took us to the police station and called our parents. My mother wasn't a big woman, but she could really deck me. Which she did. She had become both mother and father to us, which couldn't have been easy. Determined to straighten me out, she sent me to a parochial school, even though the high cost made things tight at home.

Sports saved me. The nuns at the school were pretty good athletes—no Babe Ruths but good enough—and we had a coach named Vito. Between school and Little League, I was spending a lot of time learning about competitive athletics.

I was playing soccer, baseball and football, and to be honest, I actually liked football the best; I had a good arm, and

I was a good quarterback. Third base? That didn't come until much later. I was a pitcher and shortstop first.

By the time I was a senior in high school, I was All-City for three years in both baseball and football at Franklin High School. And I had finally made the move to third base. Scouts were coming to watch me—but they were scouting for football, not baseball.

Still, baseball was my real love. Just to be near it, I got a job at the stadium where the AAA Rainiers played, and I did it all: grounds crew, mowing the lawn, ushering in the bleachers. Then I got promoted to bat boy and had the high honor of polishing Vada Pinson's shoes—he was the Cincinnati Reds' top prospect at the time. Two years later I would face him in the majors, but I didn't know that when I was putting a spit-shine on his shoes.

I had a great senior year, and as a result, I was chosen to participate in the Hearst All-Star game at the Polo Grounds in New York in 1958. It was THE premier game for high school players, bringing together the best talent from across the country. I was thrilled to go, terrified to leave home. I'd never been away from Seattle, much less to New York. And I was the only player from Washington selected. Was I that good? Was I that lucky?

I was the starting catcher for the U.S. team, playing alongside my future teammate Paul Popovich, and future Expo John Bocabella. On the other side, for the New York All-Stars, Joe Torre was playing.

We lost 9-0. I threw out one guy stealing, but I also threw a ball into centerfield and dropped a simple pop-up. Just my luck, the game was heavily scouted. Well, at least I had a couple of hits.

I guess I didn't play too badly, though, because the scouts hung around to talk to me. A Yankees scout asked me to stay in New York for a few days to work out at Yankee Stadium. The Cleveland scout asked me to stop by Ohio on my way home to Seattle so I could work out with the Indians.

I was thrilled. Still, I decided to head straight home and discuss the situation with my new father, John Constantino, whom my mother married several years after the divorce. By the time I got there, he was already being deluged with calls from scouts from every major league team. They were calling, coming to the house. It was unreal.

The Indians scout was the first to make an offer: a $50,000 bonus to sign with their Class AA team. The money was unbelievable; I couldn't even speak. Someone was going to pay me that much money to do what I loved? How could I not take it?

I didn't take it. We had a plan to talk to everyone who was interested before making a decision, and that's what we did. My father was confident we would hear from all 16 teams, and he was right. The highest offer was from the Cincinnati Reds, for $80,000, and it was tempting. I had grown up watching those AAA Rainiers, the farm club for the Reds. I knew the team. I had shined their shoes. I had even had a tryout with the team when the big league Reds came to town to play their minor league counterparts in an exhibition game. Because of my success in high school, I was invited to take batting practice against the parent team. It was an unbelievable opportunity to see major league pitching and stand on the same field as Gus Bell, Frank Robinson, Johnny Temple and Roy McMillan.

I honestly didn't know what to expect the day the Reds came to town; maybe I was brave, maybe I was naive. I just believed I could hold my own. I didn't know who I'd be facing, but I assumed it would be a coach or a pitcher who didn't see much action. I got dressed in the same clubhouse I usually cleaned, grabbed my 31-ounce bat—light by major league standards of the time—and headed out to the field.

Except that the pitcher wasn't some coach or weak-armed pitcher: it was big Don Newcombe, one of the hardest throwers in the game.

The Reds' manager, Fred Hutchinson, who went to the same high school as I did and who was a wonderful man, turned to me and told me to get into the cage. I was so nervous I could barely breathe.

The first pitch hit my fist; the second one nearly broke my bat. The catcher, Ed Bailey, who was openly laughing, tossed me a 38-ounce bat. Something about separating the men from the boys. I could hardly lift it.

Not an impressive debut.

Still, the Reds wound up being interested, and that $80,000 was sounding awfully good. But I didn't want to stay in Seattle with the AAA club; I knew it was time to go away from home. And I had plenty of other teams to choose from, since everyone had called. Everyone, that is, except the Chicago Cubs.

I was pretty surprised, too, because I had become pretty friendly with the Cubs scout, a gentleman by the name of Dave Kosher. He had scouted me heavily during high school, and I was confident he was going to come through. We waited.

Finally, he called. And he didn't sound happy. "Ron, I know what you've been offered," he said. "We can't even come close to your *lowest* offer. Hard Rock Johnson [the head scout] is offering $20,000."

I thought for a moment. "Bring him over anyway." He was shocked. "Listen," I said, "you've followed me since high school. I want to give you a shot. I owe you that."

Hard Rock was a burly, strapping man with a mean face. They didn't call him Hard Rock for nothing. "I'm not going to take your time," Hard Rock said bluntly to my father and me. "We know what you've been offered, and we're offering $20,000. There's no way you're ever going to be a third baseman in the major leagues, son. Maybe you can make it as a catcher. But that's about it." We tried to discuss his opinion, but it was pretty clear that his mind was made up.

And that was it. I drove Dave Kosher home, and he apologized for what happened, although he acknowledged he had no control over what Hard Rock did.

I couldn't be mad at him, I told him. "You've been wonderful to me…you've given me so much confidence. I really appreciate what you've done for me." I didn't say it out loud, but deep down, I was trying to keep the door open for the Cubs. You see, even though I grew up watching the Reds' system, I had an affinity for the Cubs. I loved to watch Ernie Banks, and I was intrigued by the incredibly long dry spell they had had since their last championship. And I believed I had a better chance of making it to the majors with the Cubs, since they weren't as rich in the talent department as, say, the veteran-laden Reds. Plus, I really liked Dave Kosher.

Finally, I sat down with my father to discuss our options. "Well, son, I can't believe this. I've never seen so much money in my life. But what's important to *you?* You can focus on the money or you can focus on getting to the big leagues. What's your choice?"

"I want to get to the big leagues," was the only answer I could give. And I knew I would get there faster with the hungry Cubs. I just didn't want to get lost in the maze of the minor league system, where some clubs had 20 teams in their organizations, from Class D up to the majors. Of course, today's teams have only five or six teams in their systems: fewer players to evaluate, fewer players to climb over to get to the top. These days, a decent player doesn't have to spend that much time in the farm system, and I think it shows on the field. The fundamentals aren't always there, those basic skills like hitting the cutoff man and knowing when to go from first to third on a base hit. We used to learn that stuff in the minors. Now they learn in big league stadiums.

But back then, you could spend an entire career trying to get a shot at the majors, and I wanted the fastest road possible. My mind was made up. I was signing with the Cubs. To me, $20,000 was the same as $50,000 or $80,000. It was all a lot of money. Had I known then what I know now—that I would have made it to the majors with any club—I probably would have taken the bigger check from the Reds. But I've never regretted the call I made to Dave Kosher the next day. Had it not been for him and his loyalty to me, I might have only come to Wrigley Field in a visitor's uniform.

I was going to be a Cub.

three

Diabetes

I must confess that I've always been a bit of a hypochondriac. If I felt ill in the slightest way, I was sure it was fatal. I guess I couldn't accept all the good fortune that was raining down on me. I had my family, a future in the sport I loved and $20,000 burning a hole in my pocket. I was on top of the world.

And then my bubble burst.

Before leaving for my first minor-league Cub camp, I went for my annual physical. Nothing unusual, just the regular exam. You see the doctor, you go home.

Not this time.

For the first time, the doctor looked at me with a look you never want to see from a doctor and said, "We found sugar in the urine."

What? What the heck did that mean? Big deal, right? Wrong. He told me to go straight to the hospital for a glucose tolerance test. I couldn't even pronounce it, let alone understand what it was. Finally, he tried to explain.

"Normally, Ron, when we find sugar in the urine, we suspect diabetes," he said.

The next question came without hesitation. "Will I still be able to play baseball?"

He paused, and the look on his face sent me reeling. "Well, yes," he said, hesitating, "but you'll have to learn some things about this disease."

Learn what? I didn't even know what it was. And in the 1950s, it wasn't talked about openly like it is today. Diabetes just wasn't something you heard about all the time.

I went to the hospital for the tests, and the results came back immediately: my blood sugar was over 400, which was very high. I was a diabetic.

It was unbelievable: I woke up that morning a happy, healthy teenager, and suddenly I had a disease I had never heard of. I didn't have the common symptoms—fatigue, frequent urination, weight loss, constant thirst—but I was a diabetic, no question. And no one could tell me whether I could play baseball again.

My mother had a long talk with the doctor and offered some assurance. "You're still going to play baseball," she said, "but there are going to be certain side effects and complications if you don't watch it." Great, but I didn't even know what to watch. I headed to the library.

There I sat, poring through books, trying to pick up any information I could on what was going to happen to my body. I really believed then (and still do today) that if you're afraid of something, you have to learn more about it. It's easy to be afraid of something you don't know anything about. So I wanted to know everything I possibly could, yet what I was reading wasn't making me any less afraid.

"The life expectancy of a juvenile diabetic is 25 years," I read. I was 18. "It is the number one cause of blindness, the number two cause of kidney failure, and number three cause of hardened arteries." I stopped reading. I couldn't absorb the horror.

Blindness, kidney failure, death? I was at the peak of my athletic ability—how could I be dying? How could this be happening?? At the time, the prevailing medical theory was that diabetes was strictly hereditary. I have since learned that a traumatic event in one's life can trigger the disease. I have never been able to trace a genetic link to my diabetes, and I suspect my father's leaving the family when I was seven may have had a lot to do with it.

I had decisions to make. I was scheduled to begin my new career with the Cubs; what was I going to tell them? Should I keep my secret and give myself a chance to let them judge me without prejudice? Or should I tell them up front, and risk having them look only at the disease instead of looking at the player? I just didn't know what to do.

Then I discovered a clinic in Seattle that helped me figure it out. There was a two-week program I could attend; diabetics like myself went all day to listen to lectures, meet with doctors and be monitored. The doctors would assess our conditions and offer a regimen for our treatment. Of the 25 people in the program with me, I was the youngest. Most were my mother's age.

The first week, the doctors gave it to me straight. I would need insulin to survive. Not every month or every week, but every day. For the rest of my life. There was no cure and no hope for one. I thought my life was over.

The second week, though, I thought I had it all figured out. Exercise, I learned, could help keep the blood sugar low. Aha, a way to fool the doctors. Before class, I would run hard for a while and lower my blood sugar levels; then when the doctors would test my blood, they would see how low it was and let me bypass my daily shot.

I was not going to take insulin.

As I was sitting in class contemplating my plan, the lady sitting next to me suddenly fell off her chair. The doctors immediately gave her glucose, but it was too late. She went into a coma. She was 35 years old.

After class, I asked one of the doctors what had happened—she just needed insulin, right?

"Ron, she's on insulin," he answered.

"What do you mean, she's on insulin," I stammered. "She just passed out cold. Are you telling me I could be playing third base at Wrigley Field and just pass out??"

"No," he said, "you'll have symptoms first, and you have to learn what they are. That woman has been coming here for seven years, and she still hasn't accepted that she has diabetes."

Sorry, I wasn't buying it. Any of it. Insulin, classes, symptoms, forget it. I wasn't taking shots, and I wasn't going to pass out in front of 35,000 people. Denial is part of the disease. The younger you are, the stronger the denial. I wanted to skip the rest of the program, but my mother made me stay with it. And when it was all over, I went back to that doctor, the one that warned me about the symptoms. I told him I appreciated his honesty and advice.

But, I told him, I was going to be a pro ballplayer, and pro ballplayers do not take insulin.

His answer was the same as before. "Learn your symptoms, Ron. This isn't going to be easy for you. You might walk out of here and go without insulin for a year or two. But you *are* a juvenile diabetic, and you *will* go on insulin. I know you run around the building before you come here, and I know that's why your blood sugar is low. But you will eventually be on insulin, I guarantee it."

And that was it. No room for compromise. I was just as scared as ever, but I had something just as important—

perhaps more important—to focus on: It was time to play ball. I was headed to Mesa—with my secret—to begin a new adventure.

four

Bonus Baby

I had signed as a bonus baby with the Cubs for $20,000. Now, I wasn't one of the big-time bonus babies that were inking contracts for $100,000. But believe me, $20,000 was a lot of money to me in 1959.

When the first installment of the bonus money came from the Cubs, my mother opened it and saw a check for $8,000. She gave it to me, and I can't tell you the feeling that went through me. $8,000!

I immediately put the check in my pocket, tucked a packet of cigarettes in my left T-shirt sleeve like kids did in those days and went down to our local bank.

"I'd like to make a deposit," I beamed. "I want to put $5,000 in a savings account and I want $3,000 in cash."

Ron Santo: For Love of Ivy

The teller just looked at me. Here was a Seattle teen-ager with cigarettes in his sleeve asking her to cash an $8,000 check.

"I'll have to get our vice president to come over," she explained nervously.

The V.P. came over and recognized me as one of the top high school athletes in Seattle. They did cash the check.

I took the $3,000 and stuffed it in my pants pocket and continued walking. I knew what I was looking for. I was headed straight for the local Chevy dealer.

I had decided I needed a car. Had to have one. Of course, I had never even driven one before. During high school, I rode the bus, biked or walked. Not a lot of fun when you're on a date, believe me. But there in the showroom window was a beautiful gold Chevrolet Impala convertible. It was love at first sight.

I walked into the showroom and sat myself in the driver's seat. I hadn't even touched the wheel when a salesman grabbed my shoulder.

"What the hell do you think you're doing, kid?" he asked.

"Well, I like this car and…" I got no further.

"You like this car. I bet you do. Do you have any idea how much this car costs?" he asked.

"Hmmm, well, the sticker says 3,600," I responded.

"Yeah, 3,600. That's dollars," he answered, as if I didn't know.

I proudly dipped into my pants pocket and slowly pulled out the $3,000.

"Think this will cover it?" I smiled.

They loved getting cash payments for cars back then. Suppose they still do.

So I had my car, my contract, my bonus check…now all I needed was to start my new career. I headed to Mesa, Arizona, for my first training camp.

Back in the late 1950s and early 1960s, before there

were rookie leagues and instructional leagues in the majors, the Cubs used to have a three-week rookie camp. The top prospects in the organization, those that had just signed like myself and other lower level players, would work for three weeks in Mesa, as a precursor to spring training. I had never been away from home in my life with the exception of the Hearst All-Star game in the Polo Grounds in my senior year. That was a short trip. This would be for three weeks.

I arrived in Phoenix and was picked up by Gene Lawing, who was director of player personnel. A short, stocky, unpleasant man, he drove me to the barracks we would be staying in at Mesa.

"Kid, I got to tell you, you aren't going to make it to the major leagues," were his first words to me.

It wasn't the kind of thing a nervous, 18-year-old away from home on his first long trip wanted to hear.

I was silent throughout the short trip to Mesa. I unpacked my bags, got my bunk assigned and got ready for the first day of the camp.

Elvin Tappe, a veteran catcher who was a coach at the camp, headed up the scheduled intrasquad scrimmages. Rogers Hornsby, the great Hall-of-Famer, was the hitting instructor who would be eyeing the prospects to see if we could hit.

Although I had played third base my first three years in high school, the Cubs had signed me as a catcher. I knew from the roster they had six or seven candidates at catcher including Tappe, but that's where they pegged me and that's where I thought I would have to make it.

The first day of the camp, they held an intrasquad scrimmage, and Tappe didn't play me. His only order to me was to help pick up the equipment left by the other catchers. Between Lawing and Tappe, my confidence was not exactly brimming.

The second day, same deal. There was a game between the prospects. I wasn't used.

On the third day, I decided to take some action.

"Mr. Tappe, I was just wondering when I am going to get into a game," I quietly asked.

He turned quickly, surprised that a teen-ager would ask such a question.

"Who in the hell do you think you are?" Tappe slammed back at me. "Who the hell are you? You'll play when I tell you you'll play. And no sooner."

"But Mr. Tappe, I just signed a professional contract. I was invited down here to show what I could do compared to the others. I know there are some guys here who have already played some ball, but how am I going to show you what I can do unless I play?"

"I just told you to shut up," was all that Tappe could say.

I didn't hesitate: "That's the last time you'll tell me to shut up."

And I walked away. Had I had it to do over again, I would have gone for his jaw. But for then, I walked. My prospects for reaching the Hall of Fame as a Cub didn't seem all that bright right then.

I took my spot on the bench, thinking it would be another day as a spectator for me. But then one of the young catchers got hit by a foul ball.

"Santo, get the gear on," I heard.

It was Tappe.

I didn't think about whether my challenging him had anything to do with it. I grabbed the catcher's gear and got ready for my first taste of professional ball.

During my first at-bat, I had something to prove. First swing, first at-bat—BOOM! A home run.

I was on my way.

I played every other game of that three-week camp. Hornsby worked with me, telling me where to stand in the batter's box and how to hold my hands. My disdain for Tappe was overcome by my respect for Hornsby, who at 63 years old didn't look or act anywhere near his age. Here was a guy that may have been the greatest hitter of all time, and he was working with me. I was in awe.

At the end of the camp, Hornsby instructed all of the prospects to sit on three rows of benches. I was on the second row with a young Billy Williams, who had already played a couple of years in the Cubs' lower level minor leagues. We became instant friends; I don't know why, we just had a certain chemistry.

Hornsby, in a gruff voice, looked at the first guy in the first row, much the same way a drill instructor would review his recruits. "Kid, you aren't going to ever get past Class B ball. If I were you, I'd start thinking about getting a regular job."

He went down the first row and pretty much gave the same speech.

Well, I figured, he's going to make things even worse for the second row. Then he reached Billy and paused.

"You, kid, you can hit in the big leagues."

Prophetic and accurate.

I was sweating bullets by now. What was he going to say? Would I be headed back to Seattle to look for work or doomed to a life in the sticks playing Class B ball?

He took a step over, glared me in the eye and again paused.

"And you, kid, you can hit in the big leagues TODAY."

Wow. Out of the 30 or so guys there, Hornsby picked Billy Williams and me as the only potential major leaguers.

And remember Mr. Lawing, the guy who said I didn't have a prayer? Well, he had certainly changed his tune. He wanted me to report to the Cubs' full camp.

Normally, a teen-ager would have jumped at the chance, no questions asked. But I'm a ballsy kid and told Lawing I had to go home for a week. I was homesick. I hadn't ever been away from home for more than two days, and three weeks had now passed.

The Cubs allowed me a week to go back to Seattle. I came back to Arizona and was again in awe. Armed with my monthly payment of $500, I arrived at the outside of the Cubs' clubhouse.

I had my pack of cigarettes but I realized that my puffing days might be over. How would it look for a green kid like me to come in and smoke among the heroes of the game? Top conditioned athletes would laugh in my face.

So I took one last drag off of my Lucky Strike, threw the pack down and entered the clubhouse.

Well, the smoke was so thick in that tiny clubhouse from the other guys smoking away that I could hardly see my way to my locker!

Welcome to the big leagues.

Yosh Kawano, the Cubs' clubhouse man who still holds the position, gave me number 17. I wouldn't get number 10 until the following year.

I had a good spring. Because of the plethora of catchers, I was moved to third base.

It didn't matter to me. I just wanted to succeed.

Somehow, I was around for the last cut. I was dispatched to Class AA San Antonio and was re-united with Billy Williams.

Grady Hatton, a former major league infielder who had bounced around the majors, was my first manager. I thought this would work to my advantage, having a former infielder be my first skipper.

I did little to impress him. I was throwing balls into the stands from third base. It probably wasn't safe to buy a ticket behind the dugout the way I was launching my throws. I couldn't hit much either. Hornsby's assessment several months earlier looked like a bad prediction in the eyes of the Cubs' front office which was getting the reports on me.

At one point I was hitting .169, and Hatton called me in to his office. It didn't take a genius to know what was coming.

They wanted to send me down to Class B ball. I began to sob.

"Don't send me down. I know I can come back, I just know I can. Grady, give me one week, one week, that's all. If I don't improve, just send me down, and you won't hear a peep from me." Somehow, he bought it.

I went on a tear that week, hit a couple of homers, drove in a bunch of runs. By the end of the year, I had hit .327 with 11 homers and 87 RBI. I was good enough that they sent me up to Class AAA Houston to hit in the playoffs.

I was on my way.

Filled with confidence, and still hiding the fact that I had diabetes, I approached the 1960 season with renewed confidence. Tappe's and Lawing's comments seemed a distant memory.

During that winter, I married my high school sweetheart, Judy, and we decided to have our honeymoon in Palm Springs, California. We drove that shiny gold Impala down from Seattle. Halfway through our stay, my mother called me from Washington.

"Ron, there's a letter here from the Cubs. John Holland [the team's general manager] says you're to come to Arizona as a non-roster player," my mother read.

I was beside myself. One year of pro baseball and they were giving me a shot at a regular job on a major league club at age 20.

Our honeymoon was curtailed. We headed toward Arizona.

Looking at the roster, I thought I had a chance at the regular third base job. In 1959, the Cubs used 37-year-old Alvin Dark at third, and he was clearly at the end of his career as a player. Dark would go on to serve as a coach and manager in the majors for years to come.

There were some other candidates to fill Dark's shoes, but I realistically believed I was in the running.

I had a good spring. I hit great, fielded better and did everything you would expect a veteran third baseman to do. I thought I had the job won.

Entering the final two weeks of spring training, the Dodgers came in to play us in Mesa.

Charlie Grimm, the manager, called me in to his office.

"You've had a great spring. You're going to play against the Dodgers this weekend. If you have a good series, you'll break camp with us," Grimm announced.

The pressure was on.

On Saturday, I faced Don Drysdale, who by then was one of the premier right-handers in the National League. I went 2 for 4 and made all the right plays in the field.

Sunday, I faced veteran Stan Williams, who like Drysdale was a hard thrower with plenty of savvy. I went 2 for 4 again, and one of those hits was a long home run.

After the game was over, Grimm called me in. "You can pack your bags," he said. I had a job won on the roster.

I went back to the Maricopa Inn where the Cub major leaguers stayed each spring. About 7:30 that evening, I got a call from John Holland. "Meet me in Charlie Grimm's room in five minutes," Holland said.

I'm thinking that I'm going down there to sign a major league contract for the first time in my life.

When I walked in to Grimm's room, I caught Holland's eyes for a brief moment; I knew instantly something was wrong and I wasn't there to ink a contract.

"Sit down, son," Holland ordered.

"I don't want to sit down," I answered. "What's wrong?

"We made a deal about an hour ago with the Dodgers. We traded Ron Perranowski and Johnny Goryl and $25,000 for Don Zimmer to play third base," Holland said. "Charlie and I also feel that you are a little young to be playing in the big leagues. If you get off to a bad start, that might discourage you, and we don't want that."

I immediately turned to Grimm.

"You promised me. You said I would break camp with this ballclub. Now, you're telling me you made a deal, and I'm not going to be on the major league club." I continued to make my case, pointing out my spring training stats were better than anyone's. How could they rob me of this chance?

Holland explained the deal for Zimmer, who at age 29 figured to be their anchor on the left side of the infield next to Ernie at short. Zimmer was highly thought of from his days with the Dodgers, and the Cubs believed that Zim, who would later manage the Cubs to a division title in 1989, was their man.

Both Grimm and Holland were promising me I would be back soon.

"You promised," I said, turning my back. "I quit!"

I stormed back to my room and started packing my bags. I was going home. The tears would come and go between the rage and despair I felt. I called my wife, told her I was coming home and I was through with the Cubs, through with baseball. She implored me to sit down, think a moment and re-think my decision. But I was in no mood for rational advice.

A short time later, before I could leave town, Holland came to my room.

"Ron, to show you what we think of you we're going to give you a major league contract to play Class AAA ball," said Holland.

"I don't care about the money. I can play in the big leagues," I said.

Report to Houston, he countered, and I would have my chance at the big leagues.

Between my wife and Holland's advice, I decided not to quit. It was good advice.

I went down to Houston. It was a step up, after all, from Class AA ball. Through the first half of the season, I'm hardly setting the world on fire, but my numbers weren't bad: .268 with 7 homers and 32 RBI.

On Friday, June 24, I got the call. "Ron," said John Holland, "you're to report to the Cubs in Pittsburgh for a doubleheader on Sunday, June 26."

Apparently, their plans for third base had changed. I would have run the entire way from Texas to Pennsylvania had they wanted me to.

Friday night, I'm a minor league infielder. Sunday morning, I'm the third baseman for the major league Chicago Cubs.

When I arrived at Forbes Field, one of the legendary old parks now torn down, it all seemed like a dream. I had never set foot in a major league ballpark in my life. And now, at age 20, I'm getting ready to play before 40,000 fans.

Before I went into our clubhouse to get dressed, I sat behind home plate and watched the Pirates taking batting practice.

Here were guys that I had watched and admired on television. Roberto Clemente, Bill Mazeroski, Dick Groat. These guys were no longer heroes. They were opponents.

Lou Boudreau was now the Cubs' manager. In one of the weirdest transactions in baseball history, Boudreau had come down from the broadcast booth and switched places with Charlie Grimm 17 games into the season. He later told me that had he been the manager in the spring, I would have never gone down to Houston and I would have been the starting third baseman ahead of Zimmer.

Zimmer, for his part, didn't fully comprehend the switch. He thought he was just being moved to second base for a time to replace Jerry Kendall and he might be back at third at some future time. Well, he would have had to wait until he was 44 before I would leave the Cubs and their third base spot.

The Cubs had lost nine straight games before that doubleheader. Just the day before, they had lost 7-6 and seemed headed for the basement. Boudreau started me in game one against Bob Friend, one of the premier right-handers in the league at that time who would win 18 games and along with Vernon Law would lead the Pirates to the National League pennant.

I was so nervous I'm sure I missed a lot of details of that great day, but one thing I'll never forget was the announcement from the Pirates' public address announcer: "And for the Cubs, batting sixth, Ron Santo." Goose bumps. My knees were shaking so badly as I stood in the batter's box for the first time that it must have been noticeable.

"Nervous, kid?" asked their catcher, Smokey Burgess.

I stepped out of the box for a moment. Fantasy was over. Reality was ready to set in.

Friend's first pitch to me was a big breaking ball that found its way over home plate. "Strike one," yelled the ump.

Burgess says, "Son, that is a major league curveball you just took."

I wasn't intimidated. Friend threw ball one and then another ball. Both breaking balls.

He then came back with a Friend fastball. I hit it so hard it nearly knocked him off the mound. Right up the middle, first major league hit.

I had two hits and drove in three RBI as we won 7-6.

In the nightcap, I went 1 for 3 off Vernon Law, who was 11-2 entering the game and who would wind up going 20-9. I had two more RBI on the day as we won, 7-5, sweeping the doubleheader from the first place Pirates.

First day in the majors: 3 for 7, 5 RBI. Two wins, no losses.

I didn't manage to keep up that torrid pace the rest of the year, but I had become the club's every day third baseman. The club wound up seventh, 60-94, 35 games behind the Pirates.

But on that Sunday the 26th, I thought I was playing on a championship club.

five

Moral Victories

Today's rookies, at least the highly-touted ones, are generally making more money than a lot of the veterans trying to hang on. They are confident, often cocky.

Back in 1960, rookies were the low-lives of the team. Hazing was commonplace, sometimes good-natured but often mean-spirited. We're not talking fraternity paddling here; a lot of it was mind games, much of it unnecessary.

I got my share, even after my stellar debut at Forbes Field. I wasn't afraid of a confrontation with anyone, but I knew my place. I was a rookie. Players would walk right past me and not say a word. Like I didn't exist.

An exception was Ernie Banks. Already a two-time National League MVP, Banks was a class act on and off the field. He didn't have to be: his reputation had already been established in the league. But he would come over, pat me on the rear and say, "Nice going, kid," when I needed it. It's easy to talk in superlatives about Ernie Banks; he was that type of individual.

Others didn't fall into that class.

I nearly got into some serious fights with pitchers Glen Hobbie and Dick Drott, who rode me all the time. Okay, I could take that. But when they embarrassed me in front of my teammates, I wouldn't stand for it. But no matter what, I made sure our problems stayed in the clubhouse. I have never liked anyone who aired his dirty laundry in public or through the media. That's classless.

That is not to say I didn't have a temper. The media, and I imagine a lot of fans, thought of me as a hot head on occasion. They were not totally wrong.

I sure reacted quickly to a lot of things during my playing days that I later regretted. Remember, I was only 20 when I started playing in the major leagues and I'm sure with age comes the realization you do some things you wish you had done differently. But I have always worn my feelings on my sleeve and I don't apologize for it. I'm an emotional guy now and I was an emotional guy when I was a player.

During my second year in the majors, 1961, we were playing the eventual National League pennant-winning Cincinnati Reds at Wrigley Field, facing Bob Purkey, a pretty decent right-hander who won 16 games that year. Purkey always pitched with a smirk on his face.

I was hitting only .205 at the time and struggling, so I was even more on edge than usual. Purkey started me off with a curve that I went fishing for and missed. I got back in the box and looked at him. Purkey had the smirk on his face and I took it to mean he was laughing at me.

He came back with a high fastball, and I made the cardinal mistake of being over-anxious and mad at the same time, something you don't do when you're trying to hit a 90-mile-per-hour pitch. I missed it badly again. Purkey had me down 0-2.

The smirk was still there, and I was angry. I knew we had Billy Williams at third, and my job was to get the ball into the air somehow so we got that run in from third.

Purkey then delivered a high fastball that somehow I managed to drive far enough in to center to allow Williams to score on the sacrifice fly.

As I rounded first and headed back to our dugout, I went by the mound to give Purkey a message. "Laugh that one off, you sonofabitch," I said to Purkey.

As I stepped into our dugout, I heard one of our coaches, Buck O'Neal, call to me.

"Son, there's a guy behind you," he said. "I'd turn around if I were you."

Sure enough, Purkey was coming after me.

As he approached, I swung and hit him in the head. Both benches emptied out. Your typical baseball fight. No one got hurt; no serious punches were thrown.

The next day I got to the clubhouse to dress for batting practice and was told that John Holland wanted to see me.

I made the slow walk up to his office and I felt like I had thrown chalk at the teacher and was going to have to sit in a corner. Worse yet, I thought maybe they'd send me to the minors for taunting Purkey and getting both teams into a fight.

Holland instructed me to sit down. I was ready for the worst.

"Son, I've been general manager a couple of years," he said, "and what you did yesterday picked up the club. I'd like to give you this little bonus."

He handed me a $2000 check made out to Ron Santo from the Chicago Cubs.

I felt like asking him when he wanted me to fight next. I was ready to take on Sonny Liston.

Just so you don't think my actions were the symptoms of youth, I did have a similar episode toward the end of my career. I had been tossed out of several games during my 14 years when I may not have deserved it, but there was one time they should have tossed me—but didn't.

In 1972, we faced the Dodgers at Wrigley Field. In the second inning, I led off with a solo homer off Tommy John, and we were holding a 1-0 lead when Willie Crawford came to bat for the Dodgers in the seventh.

Crawford singled, and went to third on a single by fleet Willie Davis. No outs, Bill Russell at the plate. Hickman and I played in at first and third, Beckert and Kessinger were playing back at second and short for a double play. Russell hit a grounder to Beckert, who threw home to try to prevent Crawford from scoring the tying run. Crawford was trapped in a run-down and I tagged him so hard on the butt that I thought I hurt the guy.

Third base umpire Jerry Dale yelled safe.

I went crazy. I blasted him with the only words I could think of. "You're full of shit," I screamed.

I was nuts by now. I knew Dale blew the call and that the Dodgers were set for a big inning that could win them the game.

My teammates had to do all they could to restrain me from hitting him. When I broke loose and gained some temporary sanity, I went to home plate umpire Tom Gorman. Gorman told me to cool down and he would talk to Dale, an umpire's way of brushing you off. But this time, Gorman and Dale talked and for one of the few times in my career, Gorman overruled Dale and called Crawford out at third. I felt vindicated and more importantly, we've got one out.

As I was back at third, I saw Walter Alston, the Dodgers' manager, coming out to complain. Alston wasn't running; he never ran out of the dugout no matter what the situation. He would have the same methodical steps regardless of the situation in a game. Alston walked to Dale, and I overheard the conversation.

"I know that Santo tagged Willie Crawford out and I also know that he called you a mother————," Alston said. "That's a three-day suspension, and Santo should be out of the game."

Give credit to Alston; he knew he'd lost the battle but figured he could win the war with me out of the lineup. But neither Dale nor Gorman would give me the thumb. We got out of the inning without being touched for a run, although Joe Ferguson had a two-run homer in the ninth and the Dodgers won the game 3-2.

After the game, I sat in our dugout, reflecting upon my temper tantrum—I knew I had over-reacted. I knocked on the door of the umpires' room which was located right behind our home dugout.

"I just want to apologize to you for the way I acted," I said quietly to Dale. "I was wrong." He accepted my apology.

I also went after a few managers in my time. In 1970, we were facing the Expos at the old Jarry Park, and Gene Mauch was their first manager. Mauch was a skilled player who, unfortunately, never got into the World Series. He would come close, first with the 1964 Philadelphia Phillies and later with the 1986 California Angels. It would shadow his great accomplishments just as it affected our Cubs teams of the late 1960s and early 1970s.

Mauch would constantly ride the good hitters from the bench; that was his way of trying to get our goat and gain an advantage for his team. Sometimes it worked, other times it didn't. In my case it wasn't personal. I know I probably hurt his best chance to get in the World Series in 1964 when his Phillies had a 10-game lead and blew it to the St. Louis Cardinals over the final two weeks of the season. I had a big year in the majors—my best, 30 homers, 114 RBI and a .314 batting average—and I had my best stats against Mauch's

Phillies. I was just coming into my own as a hitter: I had developed patience at the plate and was getting to know the pitchers in the league. It all came together and unfortunately for Mauch and the Phils, it came together the most against them down the stretch. Mauch never forgave me for the key hits I got down against them—I'm sure I cost the Phils a few key games.

So we were facing the Expos six years later at this old park where the dugouts were so close to home plate, anything said from the dugouts could be heard by the players and most likely the fans. During this particular game, I stepped to the plate in the second inning to face Steve Renko, a big guy with a good fastball who wasn't afraid to throw the ball inside. Renko got ahead 0-2 and I heard Mauch bellowing very clearly:

"You know what to do," Mauch yelled to Renko.

I stepped out at the plate and glared at Mauch. I knew what was coming. A "purpose pitch." I was sure it was a mind game that Mauch was playing, that he was trying to get me to look for a pitch way inside. But I didn't want to yield for fear that Renko would throw a curve on the outside part of the plate and I would be dead meat.

Well, the ball was up and away.

"Do what I told you," he again yelled to his pitcher.

Again I stepped out, only this time, I yelled back at Mauch.

"If he comes close to me I'm coming after you,"
I yelled.

I ended up walking and as I went to first, Mauch was still screaming at me. My Italian blood was starting to boil.

We didn't score, and as I went back to the dugout to get my glove, Mauch came out of his dugout and yelled at me louder.

All of a sudden, I was over the boiling point.

I made a mad dash to the Expos dugout; I wanted a

piece of Gene Mauch. It was a stupid thing to do because none of my teammates were nearby. I wasn't thinking too clearly at the time.

By the time I got to the Expos' dugout, big Dick Radatz, the former Boston Red Sox fireballer who was now with Montreal, grabbed me by the neck. Fortunately, Radatz was a buddy of mine, so he probably wound up saving my life. As Mauch and I were being restrained, he yelled at me, "You've killed me. I'm fed up with what you've done to my career!"

Meanwhile, my veins were bulging out of my neck and having a conversation about his managerial career wasn't a priority.

As we finally broke it up, the Expos' fans threw hot dogs, although I was expecting croissants. Beckert, my roommate, got hit square in the forehead with one of those Canadian weenies. He was the only reported casualty.

By 1961, after my second season, I was still not taking insulin. My weight was at 185 pounds, but I'd watch my diet carefully. The Cubs still had no idea about my problem. They would check the usual things but they didn't check the urine. I stayed off the insulin and I was still fooling them. Routine physicals weren't showing what my doctors knew back home.

After that season, my wife and I decided it was time to lay down some roots in Chicago. We found a one bedroom place within walking distance of Wrigley Field for $240 a month. That was, believe it or not, expensive for those days, and my salary was in the neighborhood of $8,000. That's per year, not per at-bat.

After we moved that fall, I started experiencing some pain in my right leg. It was getting worse and worse. Suddenly, I was losing weight for no reason. And urinating all the time. I knew what was wrong.

I contacted my son's pediatrician and told him in the strictest confidence that I was a diabetic. He referred me to another doctor. "And Ron, get there in a hurry," he said. I had suddenly dropped 22 pounds and felt myself wasting away. I knew I was in trouble.

I went immediately to the doctor. After the examination, the doctor came in with a stern look and a bottle.

"Ron, this is insulin. Take it. Take it now," he ordered. "If you don't start taking it now, you will lose that leg." I realized I had lost the battle. The Seattle doctors had been right.

The doctor ordered 15 units of insulin and told me to come to his office every other day. I told him I had not informed the Cubs of my condition. "Doc, I made the big leagues with diabetes. I know I can play here and I've proven it. I don't want people to know," I said. "I'm scared."

His plan was simple. In addition to trying to save my life, he was going to educate me about the potential problems and warning signs of diabetes. He made me take the off-season before I reported to the Cubs in 1962 to learn. After years as a begrudging student, I had to become his willing pupil. For my career, my family, my life. My teammates who saw me during that winter thought I was intentionally losing weight to gain more speed.

One week before I went to spring training, the doctor raised my dosage to 30 units. Then he told me that I was going to have to learn my symptoms. "Ron, I want you to go out to a gym with a friend. Take regular sugar with you and some orange juice, a chocolate bar and take your insulin. Eat your regular breakfast, play basketball," he said. "And wait for your first symptom. When you start to feel weak, take that sugar."

I followed his instructions. I ran up and down the floor, shot hoops. A half hour passed. Nothing, no symptoms. After about 45 minutes, I started to feel a cold sweat through me. Then I was famished.

"Time it," I said to my friend. I kept shooting baskets. Soon my tongue had no feeling.

"Time it," I again instructed.

Then my nose had no feeling.

"Time it," I ordered.

All of a sudden, I was rubber-legged. It took only 20 minutes from the first symptom to blurriness and dizziness.

I sat down and my friend gasped, "Ron, you're white."

I started slurring my words. My buddy told me to take something, anything. He thought I would go into a coma and die.

"Not yet," I managed to say. I was terrified but I had to see this through.

Finally, I looked up at the backboard above me and saw three rims. At that point, I took straight sugar hoping that would snap me out of it. Nothing happened. My body was craving more sugar. I drank some orange juice with more sugar.

Suddenly I started to feel a tingling sensation that gave me the impression I was retaining some of my faculties. I was still scared to death. After about 15 minutes, I was just about back to 100 percent. I could speak without the slur and I was starting to think rationally. Slowly, very slowly, I was coming out of it. My color returned, and I saw just one rim instead of the three. The other sensations were going away.

I immediately called the doctor to let him know what happened.

"Ron, that's all you need to know," he said. "You know now not to wait until your last symptom. Especially playing a night game and then a day game. You have to regulate your insulin. It's going to be tough, but you can do it. When you feel that very first symptom, take that candy."

He emphasized that the key was to always be cognizant of my symptoms, to always carry something with sugar, a candy bar or something, in the dugout.

"You won't be able to stay on a diet," he added. "With the traveling of baseball, day games, night games, it's going to be very important to regulate that insulin." I wasn't like a guy with a regular nine-to-five job; the challenges would be greater for me.

I went to spring training feeling more confident about my health. About that time, the Cubs hired Dr. Jacob Suker, who would serve the organization for more than three decades. I trusted Suker immediately.

"Jake, I'm a diabetic. I've been on insulin for a couple of months," I explained. "But I haven't told the Cubs yet."

Naturally, he was surprised. How had I concealed this disease from the organization?

"Jake, listen to me, I want to make my first All-Star game. It's important to me. I don't want anyone else to know about this."

He seemed to understand. I was determined that as few people as possible know about my diabetes until I made the National League All-Star team, something I did in 1963 for the first time.

I suppose it got out to some of my teammates by then; certainly to the guys I roomed with on the road. The media wasn't aware of it until 1971 when I made an announcement; if the writers knew about it before that time, they never wrote or spoke one word about it. I was glad it worked out that way. I've never been embarrassed to have the disease—I just didn't want anyone to see me go 0 for 4 and think it was because I was a diabetic.

That first season playing with the insulin was difficult. After batting .284 my sophomore year, I dipped to .227 in 1962. It would be as low as I would hit on a regular basis as a member of the Cubs. My homers dropped from 23 to 17, again, the low mark of my career. Worse yet, I made 24 errors, leading the league for the second straight season.

It was like a rookie season for me. But I learned to

make the adjustments, and by the next season, my numbers reflected it: batting average .297, 25 homers and 99 RBI. I led the league in games played and finally got to the All-Star game, something I was fortunate enough to do another eight times during my career.

As if those first years weren't difficult enough dealing with my health, they were made more difficult by the Cubs' managerial merry-go-round. Of course, managers come and managers go; it's part of baseball. But for the Cubs' front office, one manager—Lou Boudreau—wasn't enough. They decided the Cubs needed *lots* of skippers. Thus was invented the infamous College of Coaches.

There were at least 100 good reasons to try this experiment; as it turned out, there were at least 101 reasons to call it a monumental bust. Even today, when mention is made of the College of Coaches, it brings out the laughter and disrespect that was immediately associated with the Cubs teams I played on in the early 1960s.

Boudreau had sought a two-year contract extension to manage in 1961 and 1962, but Mr. Wrigley didn't like two-year contracts. For all of my seasons with the Cubs, I only had one-year contracts. Multi-year contracts just didn't exist. Boudreau wanted one and couldn't convince Mr. Wrigley to change his mind.

So Lou headed back to the broadcast booth, and the Cubs were left without a manager going into 1961. And then one of my least favorite people, Elvin Tappe, went to Mr. Wrigley and suggested the idea of the College of Coaches. Just so you know who to blame. There would be a faculty of instructors from the organization who would, in effect, run the club.

For nearly 90 years, baseball had survived with the concept of one manager. Now the Chicago Cubs were going to break with tradition.

That first spring training in Mesa under the new regime was a military boot camp. The only thing we didn't have were the khaki uniforms. Among the faculty was Col. Whitlow, who was our sergeant at arms; he would give out the duty roster and the coaches would follow it. Col. Whitlow believed the most efficient way to run an outfit was military style.

It was nuts. This was the major leagues? This was the thing I had dreamed about all my life?

We had, at the start, 12 coaches in the college; I can't even remember all of their names. We were told that every two weeks, regardless of the outcome on the field, there would be a different head coach. They would rotate in from our minor league system.

I was 21 years old, old enough to be eligible for the real army. But I wasn't going to voice my opinions; I wanted to stay in the big leagues. In the Army, you don't challenge the officers.

But it was clear we were a rudderless ship. When you don't have a manager, even a poor one you might not respect, you don't have any leadership. Players often confide in their coaches rather than their managers—who could we confide in? It was a very difficult situation for everyone. One head coach would come aboard and tell me what was expected of me; two weeks later, the next coach would tell me something different. I would listen to everyone; if it didn't make sense, it went in one ear and out the other. After a while, it was all I could do to keep my balance. I wasn't insubordinate; I just tried to get along and not get messed up at the plate or in the field.

Of the faculty, Lou Klein, Charlie Metro and Vidi Himsl (who would always carry a clipboard that he coveted) were the best of the lot. Tappe was probably the worst of the lot. We just never hit it off from day one, and it never improved. Metro clearly knew more about the game than anyone, but you did it Metro's way or you didn't do it at all. At one point,

Bob Will, our player rep at the time, got a petition to tell Mr. Wrigley to get rid of Metro. I didn't sign it, but they got rid of him anyway.

The chaos from the College of Coaches carried over to our performance in 1961 and 1962. My second season, we were ninth and lost 90 games despite my having 23 homers and 83 RBI; Ernie and Billy combined for 54 homers and 166 RBI. The next season, incredibly, it got worse. We managed to lose 103 games and actually finished behind the Houston Astros, an expansion team that was in their very first year of existence.

Unfortunately, the impact of the College of Coaches had an effect on the club that lasted longer than the college itself. It left its mark on the rest of the decade. For example, Lou Brock, a promising young outfielder in our minor league system, came up in 1962 after impressing the front office the previous year. Brock sprayed the ball all over the field and also had power. He had a good arm and a lot of speed, and I mean a lot of speed.

If our coaching system was confusing to the veterans, it was downright perplexing to rookies. Brock was getting so much advice from different people his head was spinning; like any young player, he was trying to please too many people.

Brock hit .263 that first year, and he knew he could do much better. Apparently Holland and the College of Coaches didn't think so. I knew this guy had super talent, that he was headed for stardom. They didn't.

Brock was still struggling in his second year; his head was so filled with conflicting opinions he didn't know where he was. The only thing that wasn't confusing—at least to his teammates—was that this young prospect had tremendous raw talent and great maturity.

His average was still respectable at .258, but he had struck out 122 times. He was pressing and he knew it; he couldn't use the great speed if he couldn't get to first, and he was playing a weak left field due to his confusion at the plate.

In June of 1964, we had a team golf outing. At the banquet that night, Holland and Bob Kennedy, who had now ascended to "head coach" on a permanent basis, walked in. I knew from Kennedy's face something had happened, something not positive. As captain of the team, I had enough nerve to ask him what was wrong.

"We've traded Lou Brock," he announced, looking unhappy.

"You've done WHAT!?" I said in disbelief. We had acquired Ernie Broglio, a former 20-game winner with the St. Louis Cardinals who had one of the best curve balls in the game.

Unfortunately, he also had the gout. And elbow trouble.

Broglio never helped us. All Brock did in 1964 was to lead the Cardinals to the National League flag. He was hitting over .350 with them, stealing bases left and right and playing spectacularly in the field.

He only got better. In 1967 and 1968, when we started to become contenders, Brock was as dangerous a player as there was in the league. He hit for power, caused disruption of the other team's defense with his speed and he hit for average. Could we have used him on those near-great teams later in the decade? What do you think?

Needless to say, the Broglio-Brock deal would go down as the worst in the history of the franchise and one of the worst in the history of baseball.

Kennedy had been selected as the sole head coach—okay, manager—in 1963, and he did the best he could with very limited personnel. He was a solid manager, a good baseball man and he later became general manager of the club before the arrival of the Chicago Tribune Company and Dallas Green.

We actually had some great arms in those years: Larry

Jackson, Bob Buhl, Dick Ellsworth along with Hobbie and Drott. Lindy McDaniel, the former Cardinal, was about as good as we had in a fairly weak bullpen. We seemed to have a revolving door in the pitching staff; one year in 1964 we actually had 25 different pitchers get in to at least three games for us.

Those first years with the Cubs may have been disappointing on the field, but there were some great moments. I met some great people, and while you don't love everyone on your team, you go to war for them. We had some characters on those clubs; humor was our salvation from the constant losing.

And every once in a while you meet someone who is indeed special. In my case, it was Kenny Hubbs.

Like myself, the Cubs were projecting Hubbs to be a part of their infield for the 1960s. He had great tools in the field, the best I've seen along with Ryne Sandberg. He was graceful, talented, humble. He came up to the club in 1962 as a rookie, and it was clear from the very first he would make it immediately. As it turned out, Hubbs would go on to become rookie of the year, one year after Billy Williams had copped a similar honor.

At spring training in Mesa, they made us roommates. Being a devout Mormon, he was somewhat shy and quiet but clearly an aggressive player once he took the field. The only thing he was terrified of was flying. Hubbs hated to fly, scared to death of it. To tell you the truth, I was never comfortable flying back in those days, but I coped. Not Hubbs. He was truly petrified of getting on a plane. He was a true white-knuckle flier; I found it a bit of a paradox, because here was a man so strong in his belief in the Almighty, yet he was worried about flying.

Every road trip, we had to coerce him to get on a plane. For some reason, sitting by the window would calm his fears somewhat, so whenever it was possible, we made sure he got a window seat.

Hubbs, who had a great sense of humor and at 20 was making the transition to being a major leaguer, was engaged to a Mormon girl he had met, but his parents objected to this marriage because she wasn't the "right type" of Mormon. So when he started coming in late at night, I just assumed he was dating or having a good time, especially because his engagement was being broken up.

Finally toward the end of spring training in 1963, my inquisitiveness got the best of me. "I know it's none of my business, Kenny, but I got to know. What have you been doing all these evenings?" I asked him.

"Nothing is going on, Ron, but I'll tell you this, I have a surprise for you," Hubbs teased.

As we got ready to board the plane to head back to Chicago, I knew my roommate would be going through his pre-flight nerves, and I was prepared to try to ease the pain for him. But all I noticed was how calm and serene Hubbs was. As we buckled our seat belts to get ready for takeoff, Hubbs pulled out his wallet.

What does he show me?

A flying license.

He discovered the best way to overcome his fear of flying was to actually learn how to pilot a plane and get his license.

I couldn't believe it.

"Ron, it's so great, it's like being closer to God every time I take the plane up," Hubbs explained. "It's wonderful."

After being named rookie of the year in 1962, Hubbs seemed to be the victim of the sophomore jinx. His average dipped 25 points from .260 to .235, but he remained the best fielding second baseman in the league. He never got moody or depressed when he went into a hitting slump; he just continued to improve into a solid hitter and outstanding fielder.

At the close of the 1963 season, Hubbs asked me to

join his family in California the next time I went back to Seattle to visit my family. So when I decided in December to make a short trip to Washington, I decided to take Hubbs up on his invitation.

Almost from the first minute I got there, Hubbs was bugging me to go on up in his Cessna 180 so he could show me what a skilled flier he was. I still couldn't believe someone so afraid of flying two years earlier was trying to get me to get on a plane.

We had a ball. For one hour, Kenny Hubbs, star second baseman for the Chicago Cubs, was Charles Lindbergh.

Hubbs was flying to Salt Lake City the next day, and I had to get up to Washington that same night, so Hubbs took me to the nearby airport. We shook hands, and I headed up toward Seattle.

The next day I was running some errands and I flipped on the car radio. The bulletin sent a shock wave through my system: Kenny Hubbs, second baseman for the Chicago Cubs and rookie of the year in 1962, was missing on a flight from Salt Lake City, Utah.

I called Hubbs's mother to see what I could do to help and, I suppose, to find out as much information on his disappearance as I tactfully could. His family had gathered at their home, and his mother told me they had found the wreckage of his plane in a lake.

I flew back to Colton that night. When I got there, everyone's worst fears had come true. They had found the bodies. At age 21, we had lost Kenny Hubbs.

Hubbs's father related the details: Kenny had gone to pick up his buddy who was getting married in Salt Lake City and they took off. But about 15 minutes into the flight, Hubbs realized they had forgotten something and was going to head back. The airport tower could hear him, but he had lost radio contact from them. He had radioed he had gone into a stall and he was in trouble.

I cannot relay in words the sense of loss felt by his family, his friends, the Cubs' organization and the baseball world. Here was a gifted athlete who never got to fulfill his destiny in the major leagues.

The next season, 30-year-old Joey Amalfitano had the unenviable assignment of trying to fill Hubbs's shoes. By 1965, another promising infielder in our organization, Glenn Beckert, had made it to the big leagues. Like Hubbs, he too, would become my roommate and close friend. And to this day, I still think about Kenny Hubbs and the kind of man he was.

I miss him.

six

Leo

In 1965, Bob Kennedy and Lou Klein split the managerial duties, and we were an eighth-place club. Even with Leo Durocher's hiring in 1966, we couldn't stop the bleeding. We lost 103 games in Leo's first year and wound up eight games out of NINTH place. Ken Holtzman was the only pitcher to even win in double figures.

After the College of Coaches, anything would have been better than what we had gone through. Our rudderless ship needed a strong admiral to steer us out of the muddy waters we had been in during the early years of my career. When I found out the Cubs had gone after Leo Durocher, I couldn't wait for him to arrive. He was the man, I thought, who would lead us out of the wilderness.

Durocher was already an institution before he stepped foot on Wrigley Field. Beginning with his days with the old Gashouse Gang of the Cardinals, right through the days with the Brooklyn Dodgers and New York Giants, he was one of those rarities in sport: when you mentioned the name Leo, everyone knew who you were talking about.

The College of Coaches had left things in disarray. Don't buy that baloney about a major league team not needing a manager; it does. Winning teams have winning managers. And we were a losing team with a losing system. It was a disaster for the team and the organization.

Leo's hiring in 1966 made complete sense. You could see our ballclub was coming together. You couldn't tell it by the standings or the statistics, but we had a sense. We were staying together as a unit and needed a veteran manager to build cohesiveness and make us a winner.

Still, we were the laughing stock of baseball at the time Leo arrived. When we stepped onto the field, you knew the other team was smirking. We were professionals and had pride, yet the club was so totally disorganized other professionals could sense it. It hurt. It's easy to say we were "lovable losers," but who wanted to be a loser?

Hiring a veteran manager, in my mind, was the right tonic. We knew that Leo would bring us immediate respect. Why, after all, would Leo take this job at an advanced stage of his career unless he thought there was a chance he could lead us out of the woods?

My first meeting with Leo (as our manager) came at the traditional mid-winter lunch in Chicago right after he was hired by the Wrigley family. It was a time when the players would come in from around the country, meet the media and give the usual platitudes that this upcoming year would be "different."

Leo spotted me at the luncheon and made a beeline through the crowd to talk to me. "Ron, listen, I know you're the captain of this team," Leo said, pumping my hand. "You can continue to be the captain. You're my kind of player. I've watched you for some time and I just want you to know that you're my man."

It was some feeling to have the legendary Leo Durocher give me that kind of vote of confidence. Actually, it was the second time he had given my career a mental boost.

In my second year with the Cubs, we were playing the Dodgers, and Leo was coaching third. Before the game, he came up to me and tapped me on the shoulder.

"You are going to be a big star in this game, kid," Leo said. "By the way, you might be wearing a Dodger uniform tomorrow."

Surprise and disbelief went through my brain. Geez, I thought, I wasn't ready to be traded. Why would the Cubs want to get rid of me so early in my career? I couldn't even concentrate on the game.

After the game, I started hearing about this monster trade: Ron Fairly, Frank Howard and Stan Williams for me. Just me. Fairly, a slick fielding first baseman; Williams, a solid, middle- and late-inning reliever; and Frank Howard, the 1960s' answer to Dave Kingman. For me.

You can imagine the size of my head! First, Leo predicts stardom for me and then the Dodgers are ready to swap three Dodger regulars for a second-year Cub infielder. Needless to say, that deal didn't transpire. But six years later, Leo was finally my boss.

On the first day of spring training that season, we had our traditional meeting at Rendezvous Park in Mesa. Leo walked in. "I want all of you to know one thing: I am THE manager. I am not THE coach," Leo barked. "What goes on on this field, I am in charge of. Make no mistake. What goes on in the front office is the front office's business. But on the field, I am THE boss. You have any complaints, you come to me. You have anything you want to talk about, you come to me, not the front office. Clear?"

If I had a pin somewhere in my locker, you could have heard it drop.

"Now, we have a pretty good ballclub here," added Leo, knowing that to install confidence he couldn't tell us we were horsesh–t. "Losing is a habit, gentlemen. Winning is a habit. Right now, you are in a losing habit. We need to get into a winning habit.

"We aren't an eighth place ballclub, believe me."

He was right. We finished 10th. But losing all those games under Leo left us undaunted; we knew we would get better, and Leo was the man to take us out of the basement. Leo really wasn't crazed during that difficult 1966 season when we lost all those games. He must have seen what others were seeing in the organization: that this was a team that was going to contend in a couple of years.

Now, not everyone liked Leo. Yet, from the first day with Leo as manager, we didn't feel like losers any more. When we stepped on the field with Leo as manager, we commanded respect. Leo was the kind you loved to have on your side, hated to have against you. He would protect his team, his hitters. Our pitchers would throw at someone if they threw at us. It was just automatic.

Many people have suggested that Leo was a lot of hot air, too much glitz and the kind who would stage fights with umpires so he could see his picture in the newspaper the following day. But it was my experience that when Leo went to kick dirt on an umpire, he meant it. The veins bulging out of his neck were not an act.

Leo did have a short fuse, and it was that trait that caused numerous problems in the clubhouse. Kenny Holtzman, who went on to such great success with the Oakland A's, never got along with Leo. He resented Leo, never had any respect for him or his theatrics. You have to understand that when Holtzman pitched, it was all business.

But Leo didn't think Holtzman had enough aggressiveness to be a winner in the major leagues. A look at Holtzman's record in the League Championship Series and World Series could probably answer the question as to who was right.

Ironically, Leo and Kenny would play cards all the time, but it wasn't your friendly game of gin. Leo wanted to beat Kenny all the time, and Kenny loved taking the pot away from Leo. They were angry gin games.

Leo wasn't the kind of guy you wanted to be around when you were losing, and we did do our share, particularly before the 1969 season.

He would insist that despite what was taking place on the field, his door was always open to anyone. But how many times have you heard a boss say that and then turn around and shut the door? Leo's swagger and reputation probably made it difficult for many players to take advantage of the "open door" policy. Other veterans felt that when you would go in and close the door, you got the feeling he was more interested in what he was going to say next than to what you just said.

As captain, players started coming to me, often with gripes about why they weren't playing and why another guy was. In turn, I'd go in and talk to Leo about it. Leo's answer was usually that the guy wasn't good enough to play. Then Leo would turn around and yell at the guy, " You will be in Podunk before you'll play here."

Leo didn't like team meetings. When they were called, it was usually because we weren't executing on fundamentals. Leo wasn't the kind of manager who would ride you if you were in a slump. But if you didn't hit the right cutoff man or couldn't execute a bunt, he'd be all over your ass. "Can't we catch a f——ing ball! Can't we turn the double play! Can't we hit the f——ing relay man!" Those were familiar refrains during his tenure.

Sometimes during these tirades, a player would act like Robert DeNiro in *Taxi Driver.* "Are you talking to me?" they'd ask Leo.

Mistake.

"You're f——ing right I'm talking to YOU!" and he would proceed to bury whoever was the target of his wrath.

During the 1969 near-miss, Leo kept an even keel, even during the stretch drive when the Mets overtook us. He didn't blame the players for the Mets' erasing a nine-game lead and winning the division; of course, he didn't take the blame, either.

Yet it wasn't as bad as you might think. I sensed things were going to get better. And even though we lost 103 games in 1966, there were some good personal highlights and some lighter moments during the nightmarish campaign.

I was starting to become a consistent hitter. To me, that's a true test of whether someone has made it in the major leagues. Many players can get hot for a couple of weeks then slide; doing it day in and day out is a better barometer.

I had put together a 26-game hitting streak during the season, and we were set to face the Mets and right-hander Jack Fisher. I lined a solid single up the middle to secure the 26th consecutive game and I was feeling good. My second time up, I had a fast ball ride up on me. I was looking to go the other way on this trip to the plate because the Mets always seemed to play me to pull the ball. Ron Hunt, who made a career of getting hit by pitches more than anyone else I ever saw, was shading me to the left side at second. So, I figured I would trip them up and go to right field.

Fisher's pitch came right in on me. Instead of stepping back, I stepped into the ball, something uncharacteristic of me.

Splat!

The ball hit me in the left cheekbone. I went down like a fighter. My immediate instinct, like any trained boxer, was to get up before I was out for the count. But it was no use. I couldn't get up.

My next recollection—and I couldn't tell you how much time had actually passed—was Leo hovering over me. I do, however, recall my first words as if it were yesterday.

"Leo, I'm blind," I said. "I can't see out of my left eye. I'm blind!"

"Ron, you're not blind," Leo said softly. "Your eyelid is completely shut. That's why you can't see."

I could feel the sensation of my tongue and I sensed the bone around the cheekbone was crushed.

They carried me off the field on a stretcher but before they put me in the ambulance for the short ride to Northwestern Memorial Hospital, I stopped them. "There's no way you're going to put me in that ambulance until I get a mirror. Now!" I demanded.

The reason? I wanted to see for myself what kind of shape I was in. I also wanted to make sure that I wasn't blind. You see, when you have diabetes, blindness is a constant fear, something that stays in the back of your mind.

They did show me the mirror, and it confirmed what Leo had said: my lid was completely shut, but I still could not see. It was a feeling of both relief and anguish. Relief that I could see, anguish about how awful I looked.

At the hospital, they had to wait for the swelling to go down before they could operate. The next day, they wired my cheekbone so I could move my mouth.

Who says baseball is a non-contact sport?

I missed a week of games, although I was only hospitalized for about three days. Before the club returned from a road trip, I went to the ballpark and convinced someone to throw me some batting practice. Anyone who has been hit by a baseball from Little League on up will tell you this is essential. It's like riding a horse, one of my great passions; when you fall off, you get back on immediately.

The team returned from the trip, and I was back in the

lineup. My old pal Vernon Law, the same guy who I battered when I made my rookie splash, was on the mound for the Pirates.

I went 3 for 4 with a home run, putting me at 27 games in a row with a hit, tying the legendary Hack Wilson. I only needed one more to break his record.

The second game of that July 4 doubleheader against the Pirates saw us facing Don Cardwell, who had pitched a no-hitter for the Cubs back in 1960, but who was now the enemy. The opener had gone long, and it was starting to get dark, always a concern in the days when there were no lights at Wrigley Field. I got an out the first time up, then walked in my next at bat. I knew that walks don't count in consecutive streaks, so I needed a hit to keep the streak alive.

Veteran Jocko Conlon, the home plate umpire, strolled over to me near the batting circle before my next at bat. "Ron, you better do it this time because I'm calling the game after this inning," he advised. Nice gesture.

Sure enough, Cardwell dealt me a fast ball over the middle of the plate, and I stroked it into right field for a base hit. The record was all mine with an assist to the doctors at Northwestern Memorial Hospital…and to Jocko Conlon. The record has since been broken by Jerome Walton, who was rookie of the year for the Cubs in 1989.

I have a lot of great memories from that year, despite our losing record. One night, we had just finished winning a game in Cincinnati, something that was rare for our club that year. Beckert and I, rooming together again, decided to meet Cincinnati infielder Tommy Helms for a drink at two local watering holes: The Living Room, where I first saw little Stevie Wonder play, and across the street at The Apartment which featured, yes, go-go dancers.

We were having a couple of beers, watching the dancers go at it, when three guys came in and said hello to Helms. Then they started to make some smart remarks about the Cubs and us in particular. Now, I had been in enough similar situations to know that a fight was on the horizon. Beckert and I continued to try to ignore these guys, hoping that Helms would get them out of our faces. However, one of them got in front of Beckert's view of the go-go girls and challenged him.

Beckert dove over a table and nailed the guy. I was making sure his buddies didn't jump into the ring for a battle royal, but the bartender got nervous, called the local police and yelled to us to get out of his place through a back alley.

"Roomie, we have to get out of here," I yelled at Beckert, pulling him off the guy he was pummeling.

Beckert and Helms were out the door into the alley. But for some reason, I stayed to make sure the guy Beckert had beaten to a pulp was okay. When I ascertained he was still breathing, I headed toward the door and heard the sirens. I figured I would meet up with Helms and Beckert in the alley, but instead, they were gone. Vanished. Adios. After all, they were the good baserunners; I was no Maury Wills.

As I started running down the alley, a police car pulled up. The officers came out with huge canines on leashes. I stopped dead in my tracks.

"Get your hands up against the wall!" they called out. I heard the German shepherds yelping and barking; they seemed hungry.

"Don't let those dogs get me!" I showed them my ID, and they began their interrogation.

"Were you in that bar just now?" they asked gruffly.

"Yes, sir," I replied, innocently enough, I hoped.

"Were you in a fight in that bar just now?" they continued.

"No, sir," I answered, lying through my teeth.

"Well then, what the hell were you doing in this alley?" they asked, "and why were you running?"

"I just left the bar through the alley, and it's dark," I answered. Was I smooth or what?

They brought me back into the bar and asked the guy who Beckert had beat up if I was the one involved in the fight. The guy shook his head.

I was a free man.

At this point, I was still unsure of the fate of Beckert and Helms. I went back to our hotel and expected to see my roommate. He wasn't there, but his blood-soaked sportcoat was. Naturally, I began to worry. Was he in jail, or maybe fighting off the cops in some other Cincinnati alley? I turned back and headed toward the scene of the crime, and sure enough, Beckert was by himself in the bar across the street as if nothing happened.

"Where've you been, Ron?" Beckert asked like an innocent high school freshman.

We played the next day. We lost.

We had our share of characters on that team. There was Bill Faul, a right-hander who threw from the side. He was a firm believer in self-hypnotism and was a forerunner of a latter-day spaceman, Bill Lee of the Expos and Red Sox. When he knew he was starting a game, he would take a little record player into the trainer's room as he got ready. The record he would play would help put him in a hypnotic state as it would say over and over again, "You're going to keep the baaaaaaalllllll dowwwwwwwn, you re going to keep the baaaaaalllll dowwwwwwwn. You're going to pitch loooooowwwwww and awaaaaaaay, loooowwwww and awaaaaaaaay." We would go in and watch him go into this trance. When the record would end, Faul would jump up and be super-hyper. He would get dressed quickly and be ready to start the game that instant. He was ready to play all nine positions of the doubleheader himself.

Unfortunately, the record didn't get him the Cy Young Award. He wound up 1-4 with an ERA over 5.00 and a one-way ticket out of baseball, presumably with his record player AND that record.

If 1966 was the last year of the dark ages for the Chicago Cubs, 1967 was the beginning of the Renaissance.

Much of it had to do with the arrival of Leo. He helped us gain respect after we became the laughing stock of the league. But the real reason we came out of the darkness was that the talent was there.

In 1966, we dropped 103 baseball games in one season. My numbers were decent enough that year: 30 homers, 94 RBI and a .312 batting average. But we were awful on the field that year and we knew it. It was an embarrassment, particularly when you consider we were behind two expansion teams, the Astros and the Mets. We had just one pitcher who won more than 10 games, Kenny Holtzman, who at age 20 was the stopper of the staff.

But the club was forming, and entering spring training in 1967, I felt optimistic. Okay, so how else can you feel after 103 losses?

Whether it was because of Leo's influence or a cosmic presence, I couldn't tell you. Honestly, during my first four or five years I wasn't even aware we were stuck in the depths of the second division. I wanted to succeed and make the club; I wasn't as worried about whether we finished sixth or seventh.

Yet as we reported to Mesa in the spring of '67, I could see the difference. Beckert was forming a great double play combination with Don Kessinger at short. They had now played together long enough to know each other's moves instinctively. Ernie was at first and was now comfortable there after the earlier transition from short. I knew what I could do at third and figured to be entering the prime of my career at age 27. Billy Williams was becoming the premier outfielder in the National League. And another big key, Randy Hundley, was developing behind the plate and showing some leadership at handling a young staff.

We had some holes, for sure, particularly in the outfield, but the pitching, which was terrible in 1966, was showing signs of being respectable. Holtzman was 21 with a full year under his belt. And another young right-hander who had won just six games for us in '66 was throwing bullets in the spring: Ferguson Jenkins. Jenkins would immediately become a dominant force in our rotation as well as becoming one of the two or three top pitchers in the National League. Another youngster, Rich Nye, just 22, had also made the rotation, and he gave us some balance in the rotation along with Jenkins, Joe Niekro (another 22-year-old) and Holtzman. We also were grooming Billy Hands as a starter and long reliever. Heck, our starters averaged 22 years old and our starting eight—even with Ernie at 36—had an average age of 26.

Almost from the time of spring training right up through the opening weeks of April we knew this was the beginning of something special. I didn't consciously believe we were pennant contenders in 1967 but I could see that this was a team; if we stayed together and stayed healthy, we could contend in a year or two.

It was also in 1967 that my diabetes made its presence known in a terrifying performance. I had been following my doctors' guidelines; I had developed a routine of taking my shots and watching my symptoms for several years as a big leaguer and felt in control of that disease. I was doing whatever was necessary to stay as healthy as I could.

One sunny afternoon at Wrigley Field, we were facing the Dodgers and a strong right-hander named Bill Singer, who would become one of their dominant pitchers in the late '60s. I couldn't wait to get to the park that particular day; I had been on a hot streak and that had a lot to do with my blood sugar level. You see, when I was on base a lot, I burned up that excess sugar. When I was in a slump, no bases, no extra running, excess blood sugar.

On this day, I went into my regular routine. Before the

game, I had my usual candy bar and a regular Coke, not diet. The game was moving fast; we usually had quick games with them because of their great pitching, and besides, games just didn't last as long then as they do today.

We were losing 1-0 heading into the bottom of the ninth.

Singer was masterful. He had given up just one hit and our prospects didn't appear to be too good. But we started a rally. We got two guys on with two out and Billy Williams at the plate. I was on deck, hoping to get a chance to hit.

All of a sudden, however, I looked up to centerfield and I saw three scoreboards out there. I knelt down. Warning signal.

I looked over at Durocher in the dugout. He knew that I was a diabetic but he didn't realize I was having a problem. It was a critical game situation, and I was afraid to ask Leo to take me out. And there was Billy, fouling off one pitch after another, while I was getting sicker. Honestly, I didn't care about the outcome of the ballgame at that point. I was saying to myself, "Strike out already, Billy, so I can get into the clubhouse." But there he was, one of the great hitters of the game, fouling off pitches. And then my greatest fear became reality.

Billy walked.

So I managed to walk to the plate, bases loaded, two out, 1-0 game. I wanted to gut it out so I decided to swing at whatever Singer threw. Regardless of what I saw, I was determined to swing. On Singer's first pitch, I thought I saw three balls instead of one. I swung at the middle ball: BOOM!!

It sailed over the left field wall, a grand slam. We won, 4-1. The place went nuts. All I had to do was circle the bases, and I wasn't even sure where they were. I figured, the only way to survive this was to run like hell and get it over with as fast as possible. I took off like it was the Olympic 440 relay.

Billy, expecting the usual home run trot, was

sauntering around the bases when I came tearing up behind him screaming, "Go faster!" I thought for sure I would pass out and not make it to home plate. Somehow I managed to get there but it was all a blur.

Everyone jumped on me and I turned to Beckert. He understood. My face was white; I could hardly talk. I was almost numb. All of the warning signals the doctors had warned me about for years were there. The only difference in this episode was that I was having these symptoms in front of 35,000 fans at Wrigley Field and countless others watching at home.

I managed to get out of the mob scene at home plate and struggled to our dugout on the third base side. I always kept an emergency candy bar there in case of this type of situation. I wolfed it down as quickly as I could and sat there for about five minutes. In those days, reporters would go directly to the clubhouse, so I was basically left alone in the sanctuary of our dugout. I'm sure today I couldn't have escaped the TV cameras and microphones.

I knew the reporters would wonder what I was doing so, eventually, I took a very deep breath and managed to make the trek to the clubhouse. The media was not aware that Ron Santo had nearly passed out and barely made it to home plate for that game winning grand slam. (For those keeping score, if I hadn't made it around the bases they could have sent a pinch runner in to finish my trek.) The unwritten rules for sportswriters were different then; they didn't play peek-a-boo with a player's private life, so no questions were asked on that day about what had happened.

Upon reflection on that incident, I wonder what would have happened had I broken into the major leagues 20 years later. Sure, the money would have been great, but I doubt I could have played with juvenile diabetes and been left alone about it. In 1967, the media, the fans and most of my teammates were not aware I had diabetes. When I was having a slump, no one associated it with the disease; when I was red hot, no one suggested that I was overcoming the diabetes and having a great stretch. I didn't want the sympathy; I didn't want any advantages or handicaps from having to play with diabetes. Today, every reporter in the country would write about it, and fans would call in to radio shows to debate what effect it was having on my game.

If my homer off Singer that day was symbolic of my ongoing battle with diabetes, it was also symbolic of our team's new spirit: suddenly we realized we had the ability to come from behind and win. Playing with more confidence—and talent—we vaulted from 10th and 103 losses in 1966 to third with 87 victories in 1967. I led the club with 31 homers and 98 RBI but I had plenty of support. Ernie had 23 homers and 95 RBI at age 36. Beckert batted .280, and Billy hit .278 with 28 homers and 94 RBI. And Hundley's handling of the young staff was brilliant. Fergie came into his own, winning 20 games with an ERA under 3.00, quite an achievement for a 23-year-old pitching at cozy Wrigley Field. When Fergie would go out on the mound that year, you knew he'd give you at least seven or eight innings. More often than that, he would go the distance, and ended up leading the league in complete games, which took some of the pressure off a bullpen which wasn't Hall-of-Fame material. We had something like 15 different guys in the pen that year, like veteran Curt Simmons, who had pitched for the Cardinals World Series champs in 1964 AND the Phillies pennant-winning club in 1950. Heck, I was 10 when that happened, and here is this guy in our pen. Don Larsen, the *same* Don Larsen who threw a perfect game in the World Series, was also given a shot at being a stopper as was Dick Radatz, whose fireballing days with the Red Sox were behind him.

Still, it was exciting playing on a winning team for the first time. Leo had ingrained into our minds that we could win any game on any day. It was the first time in my years in a big league uniform that I had experienced such a feeling.

Fans often underestimate the mental aspects of the game. Physically we were near the talent level of the Cardinals, who had won 101 games that year and the World Series with the likes of future Hall-of-Famers Bob Gibson, Lou Brock and Steve Carlton (who will be in shortly). Mentally, we had become champions. Even up to the last week of the '67 season, we were in a fight for second place with the Giants and with a break here or there we would have caught them.

From the end of the 1967 season until the start of spring training in 1968, the city began to change its attitude toward our club. After years of frustration, fans began to feel what we as players had already felt. Even the writers, who usually wrote our epitaph by the first of June, believed we were contenders. Some even picked us to overtake the Cardinals and win the pennant. And entering spring training in 1968, I really thought we could do it.

Our rotation was a year older and a year better. Jenkins, Hands, Niekro and Holtzman gave us four strong, young starters. Realizing our problems in the bullpen, we went out and got Phil "The Vulture" Regan from Los Angeles to give us a stopper. Regan responded with 26 saves to lead the league plus 10 wins. Even though Jenkins and Hands had a combined 31 complete games between the two of them that year, we had the added confidence to know if a starter broke down, the Vulture would swoop up and save the game. Adolpho Phillips, who had given us some speed in our outfield in 1967, figured to get better. We also got veteran Jim Hickman, a solid right-handed hitting outfield to balance out Billy in left. And the infield was the best in the business.

But 1968 almost got off to a disastrous start. Because we trained in the Phoenix area, there was a cluster of other teams in the area, meaning we didn't have to make any significant road trips like the Florida teams must do. Usually you got in your car, drove a couple of miles and you were there. However, we did have to make two trips each spring.

One to Tucson, about two hours away, and another to Yuma, a little farther.

For our trip to Tucson, Leo decided to give the regular starting eight the day off, along with a couple of other front-line pitchers. The only thing he requested was that we do a little light running while the rest of the squad was in Tucson. Essentially, it meant we would have the day off, something that was appreciated during the grind of spring training.

Whenever Billy and I had the chance, we would ride horses in the Phoenix area. It was beautiful there, and it would give us a chance to get away from baseball in the magic of the Arizona desert. When word got around we were going on this particular trip, Fergie, Beckert and pitchers Rich Nye and Bill Hands were all anxious to go along with us. I told the group we would meet at the stables around 11 A.M. We'd get our early "baseball" work done and then proceed with being cowboys for the afternoon.

The owner at the stables always gave Billy and me the best horses; we were seasoned riders and could handle the best of the lot. But I was experienced enough also to know a tenderfoot should ride the easiest horse.

"Now, you guys who have ridden, tell the owner because we'll get you coupled with the best horses," I explained to my group. "Now, if you haven't ridden, admit it, and we'll get you some tamer horses to deal with." Like choosing up sides for a playground game, we went around the group. Beckert said he had ridden, Nye and Hands admitted they hadn't. Fergie was the last to chime in but emphasized he had ridden before.

We were set for a day in the desert. We all got on our horses and headed toward a race track about one hundred yards from the stable. Billy, Fergie and I were leading the pack with our stronger horses while the others were holding back.

"Fergie, you wait here for Billy, and I'm going to get the other guys and get back here," I instructed, wanting to get the entire group to ride together as a unit. Nothing like unity on the field and in the saddle.

I was loping along, holding my horse under control, trying to get Hands, Beckert and Nye back with our group. They were moving along fine.

The next thing I knew, I heard a horse coming alongside of me, and he was a blur. I saw Fergie riding on top; he had a big smile on his face.

"Guess this guy can really ride," I thought to myself.

Seconds later, I realized Fergie ALWAYS has a smile on his face; win or lose, calm or panic, he's smiling. I put two and two together; the horse was out of control and Fergie was in trouble. Big trouble. Fergie zoomed by Beckert, Nye and Hands.

Suddenly, the horse made a sharp left turn, and the law of physics kicked in: Fergie went flying off the horse and landed flat on his back. My initial reaction was one of horror: our ace pitcher might be down for the count, and Leo would be furious. I could see the headlines:

"Jenkins out for the season, thrown off a horse, Santo being held for questioning."

I arrived on the scene first; Jenkins was moaning. He had a large bump on his leg and he was in pain. Real pain. Instead of calling an ambulance, we borrowed a panel truck from the stables and made a direct line for the local hospital.

When we got Fergie on board, I was determined to get some answers. "What the hell were you doing!? I told you not to take a high-spirited horse if you didn't know how the hell to ride!" I admonished him. "What were you thinking?"

Between moans, Fergie managed to answer. "When I turned him to follow you, I told him to stay. But then he just took off on me. I thought I was under control because I was yelling 'whoa,'" Fergie explained in a soft voice.

"You can yell 'whoa' all you want but unless you have the reins it won't mean a damn thing," I shouted.

We got Fergie to the emergency room, positive he had a broken leg. I was also thinking—what the hell am I going to tell Leo? He's going to go nuts!

Eventually, Fergie emerged from the emergency room with that same silly smile on his face. "Told you I had everything under control," Fergie said, maintaining his innocence.

"Fly [his nickname], jeez, why didn't you just admit it? Now your leg is busted and you can't pitch," I said.

Minutes later, the doctor came out. "The good news is that nothing is broken. The bad news is that he just has to be off that leg for at least a week," the doctor said.

"Oh, shit," was all I could say.

We got back to the Ramada Inn in Scottsdale where the Cubs stayed that spring, and I rehearsed what the captain of the Cubs was going to say to the team manager upon his return from Tucson with the rest of the squad. Shakespeare had it easy in comparison.

I developed a plan. I told Fergie he would have to call Leo himself first and tell him he went riding and bruised his leg. "I'll be here with you, but don't tell him you were with me when you got hurt," I instructed.

About 7:15 P.M. that night, I went back to Fergie's room, and we called Leo. "Skip, I had a little accident today," were Fergie's first words of this dreaded call. He then proceeded to take the phone from his ear because of the loud sound emerging from the other side.

"What, what the f—— happened?" Leo screamed.

"I went horseback riding, bruised my leg and I'll be off my feet for a couple of days," Jenkins said quietly, as if that were going to calm Leo down.

Again, he took the phone away from his ear.

"You did WHAT!?" Leo screamed. "Were you with Santo today?"

"Yes," Jenkins conceded.

I am cooked.

"The f——ing captain of this team takes the star pitcher out, and this is what happens?!" Leo yelled.

I was scared to death to face Leo the next afternoon at the ballpark. I arrived early as usual and was playing hide-and-seek to avoid having to see him. Fortunately, his door was shut in the clubhouse, but I knew I'd have to go by it eventually. As I tiptoed past the door, I heard him shout:

"SANTO, GET YOUR ASS IN HERE!"

Everyone in the clubhouse stopped talking; I guess when Mount Saint Leo is about to erupt you don't want to be caught in the lava flow.

I walked slowly into his office and sat down. I knew what was coming.

"You know, I give you a f——ing off day. You are the captain of this f——ing club and you take our star pitcher horseback riding," Leo barked. "He's going to miss opening day thanks to you. There will be no more days off for you, Santo. I don't care if we're going to Podunk with the rookies, you're going with us."

Did you ever see a cartoon where everyone is listening with one ear to the door and then they all fall in when the door opens? That's what happened in the locker room as I left.

I slumped back to my locker and Leo emerged from his office. He announced the club was going to have a meeting in five minutes, I guess to tell everyone what they had already heard through his door.

Leo started the meeting and pointed to me. "This is the captain of this team," he said. "Now, how many of you guys went riding?"

The hands go up very slowly, sheepishly.

I expected more lava but at that very moment, a figure came through the door of the clubhouse. It was Ferguson Jenkins. No cane, no limp. Somehow, his Canadian blood had overcome the near disaster of the previous 24 hours. He walked to his locker, got dressed and got ready for the day's work without saying a word.

Two footnotes:

Fergie did start for us opening day that year. He won 20 games for us. He didn't miss a start.

Also, I DID make all of the Podunk spring training trips throughout Leo's tenure with the club.

That 1968 season was an unusual one for baseball. Ernie, Billy and myself combined for something like 95 homers and close to 260 RBI. We were an awesome threesome. I mention this because 1968 was the "year of the pitcher": the mound had been lowered and pitchers dominated that season. Bob Gibson had an ERA that year of 1.12. To comprehend the numbers is almost unthinkable: to allow just one run per outing for something like 40 outings is truly one of the remarkable pitching feats of my era.

We had guys with career numbers. Fergie, despite the riding mishap, won 20 again and had an ERA of around 2.60. He struck out 266 batters in 308 innings. Unbelievable. Everywhere around the league that year there were one or two pitchers per club who were overpowering, dominant. Besides Gibson, Juan Marichal of the Giants won 26 games for his second place team. Even pitchers on second division teams were awesome. Don Drysdale won just 14 games with an era of 2.15! Chris Short won 19 with an ERA of less than 3.00 for the eighth place Phillies. And a couple of guys I hadn't even heard of before the season were tearing things up in New York: Jerry Koosman and Tom Seaver would combine for 35 wins on a club that won only 73 games and finished 11 games behind us!

We hit only .242 as a team and I fell to .246. But we didn't have a .300 hitter on the club that year, and in the entire league, there were only four guys who were able to hit over .300.

But if there was a bright side, the year of the pitcher probably helped boost the confidence of our young staff more than it demoralized our veteran infield.

We were in the race for most of that summer, fighting the Cardinals for first. That gave us an extra rush because of the long-standing rivalry we had with St. Louis. In the end, though, the Cardinals were just too strong. With Gibson having the kind of year he had and the rest like Brock, Flood, Cepeda and Roger Maris, who was playing in his last major league season, the Redbirds won again. I was surprised they didn't win a second consecutive World Series title. They lost to Detroit in a seven-game series.

I wasn't disappointed with our team, though. For the second straight year, we were above .500 and again in a pennant race. We won 84 games, fewer than the year before, but strangely I felt more satisfied with our progress after that year. I knew something special was around the corner. I just *knew* that 1969 would be our year.

seven

1969

Even with our improvement, I confess that I never had the feeling that we were certain to win every game in 1967 or 1968. If we got this break or that break, or this happened right or that happened right, we'd come up a winner. When the Dodgers or Giants would come in to Wrigley Field, there was a sense they had the guns to beat us every time. They were the front-runners in the league with the likes of Drysdale and Koufax, Mays and Marichal.

That all changed in 1969.

Every time I went out there I thought we would win. Every game. It wouldn't make any difference who we were playing or who was pitching. We knew we would whip their asses.

Going into the season, things were already different in the National League. Expansion had caused divisional alignment. Geographically, it made little sense with us and the Cardinals in the National League East while the Cincinnati Reds and Atlanta Braves were in the West. But Mr. Wrigley along with August Busch, the beer baron, didn't want to split up our rivalry. It was the best in the league. It did mean we wouldn't see the Dodgers or Giants as much, but as long as we had the 18 games against the Cardinals, I suppose our front office was happy.

With Montreal and San Diego coming into the league, it meant a trip to Canada and an extra series on the West Coast. Nothing more, nothing less. But the way we felt in spring training, we could be playing in Manchuria and we would be winning.

It's difficult for today's Mets and Cubs fans to understand there wasn't an intense rivalry between our two clubs in 1969. The Mets, after all, had been losers for the first six years of their existence. We hardly were setting the world on fire but in 1967 and 1968, WE were the club of the future, not the Mets.

There were few roster decisions to make about 1969 in Mesa. Unlike previous years, our rotation was fairly set and our everyday lineup had been playing together for a long time. That was the key to my optimism; we were veterans with the chemistry needed to finally get over the hump. Heading north for the season opener, my optimism had carried over to everyone including the media. The Cardinals, who had acquired veteran Vada Pinson to replace the retired Roger Maris, were the team to beat in our division. But instead of nine other clubs to worry about, we had just the other five teams in our division. The Cardinals, I suspected, could be had.

On Opening Day, we faced the Philadelphia Phillies at Wrigley Field. Willie Smith, a 30-year-old veteran pinch hitter, hit a homer in the 10th inning, and we won the first game in dramatic fashion. There were three teams in our division tied for first that day but from that point on we were always in first place.

We were white hot: our record was 11-1 after beating the Expos in the second game of a series up in Canada. Our start only confirmed what I had felt going into this season, and we were playing with a confidence that was unprecedented for us as a unit. Even when we cooled off a bit, we came back to put together a stretch where we won 22 of 32 games into early June. We were a close-knit group and were getting closer; we had played together for the past five years. We would work together, play together. Sometimes after games we would sit in the clubhouse for a couple of hours drinking beer and talking. And my new house in suburban Glenview became a focal point of many of our nocturnal gatherings after games.

I lived right off a lake, and one night, Billy Williams came into the pool room holding something under his arm. "Hey Bill, what you got there?" I asked, mildly curious.

It turned out Williams had taken a goose from the local pond and brought it into my new house—a house, I might add, that had a brand new rug.

"Hey, you better be careful with that thing," I warned him. "You never know what a goose is going to do."

Well, the goose probably had Mexican food the night before, because he came down with a severe case of the runs; it was all over the walls, the rugs and the floor. My wife walked down and saw the mess. Let's just say the 1969 Cubs and Hall-of-Famer Billy Williams were not at the top of the scoreboard that night.

We had bought this house in the Valley Lo subdivision in Glenview, and it used up a large amount of the Santo monetary reserves. I was making $80,000 a year then, and we just decided this was the house we wanted despite the stiff asking price. I told my wife that we would buy the house and furnish it later. When we started to win seemingly every day for the first three months, I told Judy we would be able to furnish the dining room with the money we'd be getting as part of our league championship series and World Series shares. As it turned out, it took us several years to finally complete furnishing that dining room.

We were especially close to the Beckerts, who were building a home of their own down the road in Palatine. He had been my roommate on the road, but the friendship went beyond that. He and his wife, Mary, would often get into "spirited discussions" when they would come over to our house. She wasn't your typical Hollywood image of the baseball wife; she didn't take any crap from anybody. When they first met, Beckert couldn't have gotten too many bets from his teammates that the relationship would last. She was that tough. I'm happy to say they are still married and still very close friends of mine.

The summer of 1969 was a turbulent one in the country: the war in Vietnam was at its height; the country was still getting over the trauma of the assassinations the year before of Bobby Kennedy and Martin Luther King. And we were trying to land a man on the moon.

The day Apollo 11 landed on the Sea of Tranquility and Neil Armstrong became the first man to set foot on the lunar surface, we had a doubleheader in Philadelphia. Fergie won the first game in typical Jenkins fashion, 1-0. A quick, well played game. We're riding high, 21 games over .500 and in first place.

Dick Selma, a hard thrower whom we had acquired from San Diego in a key early season deal, got the call for the second game. Selma had fit into our veteran team immediately. He looked like the Hunchback of Notre Dame—

his right shoulder was a lot bigger than his left, due, I suspect, to all the innings he threw— but we called him "Moonie" because he would space out on you sometimes. He had a great sense of humor and was the kind of guy you needed on your team to keep everyone loose.

Midway through the game, I was sitting next to Selma, and he suddenly turned to me.

"Ron, guess what? You know that a man is on the moon right now?" Selma nonchalantly said.

Well, nothing against NASA or the accomplishment, but I wasn't thinking about moon rocks; I was thinking about holding the lead and getting out of town with a doubleheader sweep. "How can you be thinking about men on the moon and not thinking about this game?" I snapped. "Moonie, get your mind off the moon and on these hitters!" I guess Selma quit thinking about the Eagle and started thinking about the Phils, because we won that game 6-1 and headed back to Chicago. It was one small step for the Cubs, one giant leap for Dick Selma.

Selma would be one of the leading cheerleaders on the club in both the clubhouse and in the bullpen. The left field bleacher fans, affectionately and now more widely known as the bleacher bums, responded to Selma's waving a white towel from the bullpen to get the crowd going.

Not that the fans in the left field bleachers needed much encouragement. They were rabid and loud: they actually became the 10th man on the field for us in 1969, a rarity in baseball. In football, basketball or hockey, the crowd usually plays a larger role for the home team than in baseball. Not in 1969 at Wrigley Field; I truly believe to this day they were a catalyst for our success from Opening Day on. We actually knew these fans; they would line up three to four hours before the game to buy their tickets and they would sit in the same spot every game riding the other team's left fielder to distraction; they would lead cheers that would spread out throughout the entire ballpark.

People weren't talking politics, war or economics the summer of 1969 in Chicago; they were talking about the Chicago Cubs. We were treated like rock stars; we would have to fight through the crowds just to get to our cars *three hours* after the game. Some athletes will tell you they don't care for that kind of adulation; we ate it up. We loved the fans; they loved us. People finally believed it could really happen—that we could win. The Cubs had been strong starters before, only to be betrayed by the ravages of inadequate talent, bad breaks or superior opponents. Some argued that our lack of night baseball left us languishing in the hot August sun and caused the perennial slide, something I never subscribed to. Others suggested Durocher played the starters too much; well, why not put the top eight guys out there all of the time?

Heading into early June, we were ahead of the defending National League champion Cardinals by a couple of games. We had a doubleheader set for Montreal and we knew the Redbirds were beginning to put their act together. When we dropped the opener of that twin bill, we knew that if we lost the nightcap, we would fall out of first place for the first time all year.

Trailing 3-1 to the expansion Expos, I was giving in to negative thoughts. Then Jim Hickman, the oldest starter on the club other than Ernie, came up in the bottom of the ninth with two outs and two on. Hickman had never received big attention for his hitting, particularly for the way he could hit the long ball—maybe that's because he played on the same team as a Billy Williams or an Ernie Banks. But on this day, Hickman was Babe Ruth. He hit a towering home run to left field, giving us a 4-3 victory and allowing us to stay in first place.

There may have been another time in my career when I was more excited, but if so, I can't remember it. When Hickman arrived at home plate, there was the usual mob scene congratulating him. But I was leading the pack, pounding on his helmet, hugging, slugging, yelling and screaming like a Little Leaguer. Hickman later told me he had a migraine headache from the pounding he took from me.

For some reason, and to this day I don't know what was going through my mind at the time, I ran down the left field line, listening to the cheers from the fans, and for no particular reason, I jumped into the air—and clicked my heels. It was a reaction. It was out of jubilation. One click of the heels from an emotional Italian. I had never done that before—ever. Little did I realize it would be associated with me for the rest of my life.

The clubhouse was a madhouse. Unlike today when players shower and get out as quickly as possible, we would stay around and talk for hours. We kept reliving Hickman's hit and the wonderful feeling of being in first place, putting down one beer after another. It was the same as I'm sure thousands of Cubs' fans did that day at their local tavern or saloon.

Late into the evening I finally got dressed and left the ballpark. As is usually the case, there were still some die-hards waiting for autographs in the dark outside of this legendary old ballpark. I would have signed all night.

When I finally arrived home, I kicked off my shoes and tuned in the news on Channel 9, WGN, just like I always did. They did all of our games, and it was a ritual to watch our game highlights on the early evening news. When I flipped on the TV, I was expecting the usual news—Nixon, Vietnam, moon voyages—before the sports. So imagine my surprise when the very first picture on the news was—*me, running down the line, clicking my heels*. Ron Santo's acrobatics were the lead story!

The next day when I arrived at the ballpark, I was swarmed by a chorus of players, reporters and fans asking me about my postgame show. Not about Hickman, not about us winning the game or staying in first place; just the

Santo heel-click.

Even Leo came down from his office and approached me. Leo could go one of two ways. On the one side, here was a man who was famous for leaping up and down hysterically along the third base line when Bobby Thomson hit the "homer heard 'round the world" in the 1951 playoffs that allowed his team to get into the World Series. On the other hand, Leo didn't like giving the opponents any ammunition to defeat him. He didn't approve of showing up the other guy or pouring dirt on anyone's face when he was down.

"Golly, Ron, this has been an exciting year, hasn't it?" Leo said smoothly.

Am I being set up? Or is he on the level?

"I've got an idea, Ron. Why don't you make this little clicking bit our victory symbol?" Leo suggested.

I couldn't believe it. "Skip, to be honest, I don't even know if I can do it again."

"Just at home," Leo added in a fatherly voice. "Just at home. I think it would be dynamite."

I had misgivings beyond the physical requirements. How would it be perceived by my teammates, the media and most importantly, the opposition? Yet I had a confidence about myself and the 1969 Cubs. We were good and we knew it. I thought, Why not?

We won that day. After the top of the ninth, I made a beeline for the left field line. I clicked not once, not twice, but three times.

A tradition was born. I knew the Cub fans were eating it up. Years of frustration, having to take the slings and arrows of the baseball establishment; well, they went nuts every time I did it.

The rest of the league wasn't so enthralled. Once they started catching on to my act, the fastballs seemed to get a lot closer to my head. The brush back pitches seemed to come much closer to my chin. The curve balls would seem to break much sharper toward vital parts of my body. I understood. I accepted it. I never minded being brushed back, especially if the Chicago Cubs were in first place and seemingly headed for the pennant. Let them throw at me, high spike me at third, say what they want. We were in first place.

I think the Cardinals were the first to visibly show their disgust with my bit. Veteran catcher Tim McCarver, now a CBS broadcaster who I considered a friend, told me during batting practice what he was hearing around the league. "Say, Ron," McCarver said as he stepped up to me around the cage, "a lot of guys around the league know what you're doing and they don't like it."

"Tim, I'm aware of it but I'm not doing it to show off. I'm doing it to excite people in Chicago," I countered during some practice swings outside of the cage. During the game, I felt a fastball whiz past my chin. No coincidence. I didn't mind; I understood. I realized some people thought it was hot-dogging, but it wasn't meant to rub anyone's nose in anything.

By July, we had about a seven-game lead over the Mets. The third place and defending NL champ Cardinals were right behind them as we headed into a three-game set against the Mets at Shea Stadium. We had just dropped three games in St. Louis but we were still the front runners.

From the moment I got into our hotel in the Big Apple, all I heard or read about was the Mets. The Mets just did this or the Mets just did that. You would have thought they were writing about the 1927 Yankees, the way the media had fallen in love with these guys. I knew they had great potential pitching—Koosman and Seaver were on the verge of becoming dominant although some guy named Nolan Ryan hadn't shown me much—but their lineup couldn't hold a candle to ours.

Veteran New York beat writer Dick Young, whom I had respected as one of the top writers in the nation, cornered me in the visiting clubhouse before the start of the first game.

"Well, Ron, what do you think of the Mets?" was Young's first question.

"Are you trying to compare the Mets to the Cubs? C'mon," I said with a deliberate sarcastic tone. "Man for man, there's no comparison, Dick. None. You've got the pitchers but don't try to compare the Mets to the Chicago Cubs."

Maybe I knew it then, maybe I didn't. I realized saying that to someone like Young was a mistake. The clicking of the heels was one thing; it was done in the safe haven of Wrigley Field. Going into the other guy's territory and telling a hot shot writer like Young we shouldn't be compared to his team wasn't the most tactful way to support Leo's philosophy of proving it on the field.

The Mets insisted that those comments inspired their second-half charge. They even did some heel clicking of their own down the stretch. Was that what motivated them? C'mon! If they needed motivation to win from a newspaper article, it makes you wonder.

We were in first place on August 19 when we got set to play Atlanta. Things were great. We had an eight-game lead, and I thought about how crazy Chicago was going to be with the very real possibility of postseason play. Kenny Holtzman, who many scouts said would be the next Sandy Koufax, was on the mound for us. In the first inning with the wind blowing in, I slammed a three-run homer off Phil Niekro, who had given me fits throughout my career with his dancing knuckleball. It would be the only round tripper I had off him in my 14 years in the major leagues.

Holtzman had great control on this day; his curveball was breaking off the plate and his 90-mile-per-hour-plus fastball was just dynamite. And he had a no hitter going when Hank Aaron stepped up to the plate for his second at-bat of the game. We were leading 3-0, but Aaron would have to be the top guy you would fear in this situation. He flexed those famous wrists of his, and I put my head down, not wanting to see the ball go out of the ballpark or the look on Holtzman's face.

When I finally turned my head, I saw Williams race toward the warning track, go against the wall and look up. He saw the ball go out of the park and put his head back down. The next instant, he looked up again, and magically, the howling winds had kept Aaron's towering drive from leaving the park! Williams made the catch and the no-hitter stayed intact.

In the ninth with two out, Aaron again stepped to the plate. I said to myself, "Why does it have to be Aaron?" I also thought what every major league quietly prays for in this situation: "Lord, if the ball is hit to me please let me knock it down" because you don't want to be the guy who screws up a no-hitter.

The ball, thankfully, was hit to the opposite field. It seemed like it took an eternity to reach Beckert at second. He got down on one knee to make sure he knocked it down, just like I would have. For some reason, it seemed like he waited a week—just like Manny Trillo used to do with the Cubs and Phillies—before he threw to Ernie Banks at first. Holtzman had his no-hitter. I was going nuts. I was absolutely convinced at that moment that the baseball gods were smiling on the Chicago Cubs and that we would finally win the pennant.

And then, suddenly, we started to tail off at home where we had been so dominant all year. After the Holtzman no-hitter, we lost seven of the next nine on the homestand.

I'll admit we were starting to watch the scoreboard; even though we were playing decent baseball, every time I looked up on the scoreboard the Mets were somehow winning. They had these two makeup doubleheaders against San Diego right around the Holtzman gem and they beat the Padres four times within 48 hours. They danced on the first-year expansion Padres that year to the tune of 11 out of 12 times.

We did rebound after the disappointing homestand,

sweeping three from the Braves and splitting two in Cincinnati all on the road. And then, we headed home for a three-game set with the Pittsburgh Pirates.

The first game of the series, Steve Blass, who led the Pirates with 14 wins that year, beat Holtzman. By this time, I was starting to get alarmed; the Mets were red hot, and I felt like we couldn't afford to lose any games.

The next afternoon, we had Fergie on the mound. I felt my usual confidence in him. It was a cold, raw September day with the wind blowing in—truly a pitcher's day. Fergie was outstanding, but so was Pittsburgh southpaw Bob Veale. We took a 1-0 lead into the ninth. Fergie got the first two outs, but then Willie Stargell took a 1-2 fastball that would have required a cannon to hit it out of the park. Sure enough; Stargell blasted it on to Sheffield Avenue against the gale. We were tied. For the first time in this magical season, I felt the confidence and momentum sliding away. I suspected others on the team were experiencing the same feeling.

The Pirates went on to win in extra innings, 4-1.

To me, that was the pivotal game of the 1969 season. You could hear a pin drop as we walked into the clubhouse. Everyone's head was down. Nobody said a word. Our usual routine of staying around and talking about the game was abandoned; we got out of there as quickly as possible.

My mood didn't change the next day when the Pirates again beat us in extra innings. We now had a four-game losing streak heading into Shea Stadium to face the New York Mets. Our lead was down to $3^1/_2$ games; worse yet, we weren't playing good baseball. The big hits that were common during the first five months weren't coming: suddenly, our big bats weren't producing. And the New York fans and media were waiting for us. They were streaking; we were in a slump. Our eight-game lead had all but vanished, and they had their two aces, Jerry Koosman and Tom Seaver, set to face us. Not the duo you want to see when the club isn't hitting.

The first game of the series was on a dreary night; it was raining off and on, and the sellout crowd of 43,000 was waving white handkerchiefs and sending out a chorus of "Goodbye Leo, Goodbye Leo," to the tune of "Goodnight, Ladies."

Bill Hands faced Koosman. We went out 1-2-3 in the first inning. Tommy Agee led off the frame for the Mets, and the first pitch came under his chin, knocking him down. I didn't hear anyone mention in the pregame meeting that Hands's first delivery should be a "purpose" pitch. Hands was the kind of guy who would let you know if he had something special in mind. So in the second inning, I'm not looking for any retaliation; why should I? I knew that Hands was not deliberately throwing at Agee. The first pitch from Koosman was inside, but not at my head. Instead of turning my back, I turned into it and it hit my wrist. I walked down to first base. By the next time up, I could hardly grip the bat. Leo took me out of the game. I had quick x-rays taken which showed I just had a bruise; I was back in the lineup. The next day a newspaper article claimed that Koosman was deliberately throwing at me to get even with Hands allegedly throwing at Agee.

That night, I was in the on-deck circle waiting to face Koosman. I was studying Billy Williams at the plate when all of a sudden, a *black cat* jumped out of the third base stands! He ran in front of me, stopped to stare and headed toward our dugout, where he glared at Leo, who was stooped on the front step of the dugout. Then he headed back into the stands.

I don't like to walk under ladders; I throw salt over my shoulder and don't light three cigarettes on one match. I especially don't like black cats in my path.

We lost the game 3-2. The division lead was down to 2½ games and the mood in the clubhouse wasn't getting any better. Still, we were in first place, but the lead was shrinking.

The next night it only got worse. Jenkins was coming back on two days rest and had to face Tom Seaver, who was perfect until two out in the ninth when Jimmy Qualls, who was being used in place of Don Young, pinch-hit to spoil the bid for history. We lost anyway.

Our mood was never worse; even though we had the lead we knew we would have to at least split the next series with the Phillies to keep the momentum and stay in first. The bus ride to Philadelphia seemed like it was a cross country trip; I kept company with a few beers as we all seemed to keep our thoughts to ourselves.

The losing streak was now at six as we limped into Philly, a club struggling to stay ahead of the first-year Montreal Expos. The Phillies, who wound up 37 games out of first place, swept the two-game series; our bats remained comatose.

Typical of the way things were going was a play we had on during the final game of that awful road trip. We were leading 3-1, and Selma, all business on this day, is on the mound in relief. The Phils got two runners on, and Selma put on a play where he was going to turn and throw to me to try to pick off the runner. It's a 3-2 pitch to Dick Allen, and he put on this pre-set sign that the coaches had installed during spring training.

"Ronnie, knock it down!" Selma yelled to me. That was the sign the play was on.

I missed the sign. Sure, I'm thinking—knock the ball down. I had forgotten that was the signal for the play. Selma wheeled and threw toward me; the ball went over my head and soared out to left field. A run scored; the Phillies went on to win that game. We were out of first for good.

Durocher went nuts. Selma was so afraid of what Leo might do he wouldn't go into the clubhouse after the game. On September 11, 1969, after spending the season in first place, we fell out of the lead for the first time. We never occupied that space again.

We ended the eight-game losing streak at St. Louis as

Hands, who was our most effective pitcher down the stretch, beat the Cardinals 5-1. But then we lost three more in a row, including a game at Montreal. By then the Mets had built a comfortable lead, and worse yet, we had two games remaining with them to try to chip away at their increasing lead.

The mistake many people make is that we folded up our tents and disappeared; that's wrong. In the final two weeks of the season, we played .500 ball, something the pundits said was all we would have had to do in the month of September to win the division. What the experts did not foresee was the Mets winning 35 out of their final 49 games.

An eight-game Chicago Cub lead had vanished and turned in to an eight-game New York Met lead.

It has also become fashionable to say we were tired down the stretch. That isn't true. The adrenaline alone of being in a pennant race kept us going; I know it did for me. They would have had to get a grenade to get me out of that lineup that year. There was just no way.

If we did have an Achilles heel that year it was our bench. We weren't as deep as we would have liked to have been. But like I said, why would you not want to put your best eight players out there everyday? Durocher kept doing that because he wanted us to lengthen our lead, not coast on it. He didn't manage that way and I didn't play that way.

Ironically, the Mets actually finished their regular season at Wrigley in two meaningless games we split. While they were preparing for the playoffs against the Atlanta Braves, we were preparing for the off-season. It was a gloomy scenario after a terrific season. People to this day continue to ask me how depressing 1969 was; it wasn't. It was a wonderful experience and a great team. I was even able to joke about it in a Chevrolet ad in 1992. I was playing a talk show host who answered "caller" questions about just about everything under the sun, like how to get out chocolate stains to anything else you could imagine. Then, a "caller" asked,

"Say Ron, what happened in '69?"

"Man landed on the moon," I replied, then wrapped up my pitch for Chevrolets.

The final tally: 92 wins, the most since the 98 won by the pennant-winning team of 1945. My numbers: 123 RBI, second to Willie McCovey's 126; 29 homers, tops on our club. My batting average: 289.

The only thing on my mind after that final game was to get out of town. The Beckerts and Santos headed to Las Vegas at the Flamingo Hotel. I did not care to watch the Mets beat the Braves in the first-ever League Championship Series. I had had enough of watching the Mets win in September.

Beckert and I tried our luck at the blackjack table, hoping to catch a glimpse of a stage show in front of us. Large curtains opened up, and instead of a chorus of showgirls, we saw a huge movie screen. They weren't showing *Bonnie and Clyde*. It was the *World Series* between the Mets and the Baltimore Orioles, just what we wanted to see. We must have been the only two rooting for the Orioles; everyone else was cheering for the "Miracle Mets."

The Orioles did win the game, and NBC asked outfielder Frank Robinson, "What did you think, Frank?"

"How did this team ever get into the World Series?" Robinson answered.

Beckert and I looked at each other at the same time: That was the wrong thing to say, Frank. The Mets, as history has chronicled, won the next four games and were the World Champions of baseball. The outcome didn't change my opinion: we were better than the Mets but the Orioles were better than both of us.

Give credit to the Mets; they won it all without having the best lineup in the league. Ed Kranepool was an average ballplayer at first; Ron Swoboda made one great catch in the World Series and everyone thinks he's Roberto Clemente. Al Weis hit a pair of homers in the World Series and he's Babe

Ruth? Cleon Jones and Tommy Agee were quality ballplayers that could start on nearly every team in the league. The key was their pitching, even though I thought our starters were just as good that season.

Then, how did they win? How did they come from eight back and beat us and then beat the Orioles?

That's a good question. I wish I knew.

eight

Don Young

Any athlete who tells you he can blot out the crowd noise, the haunting sound of the boos, the jeers, the profanities from upset fans, is just plain lying. Athletes are human. Maybe the salaries and adulation make it easy for the public to perceive athletes as non-feeling robots. It isn't true.

At the start of the 1969 season, we believed we were on the threshold of something special. During spring training, Leo called me over.

"We've got a guy, Don Young, who can be a pretty good player for us. He's young, he's raw, but he's going to be our center fielder," Leo told me in his usual teacher-student voice. "Tell you what I want you to do, Ron. Take him under your wing. Help him. The only thing we don't have this year is a center fielder. This kid is a different type of kid but he can catch the ball, has good speed and a pretty good arm.

"I want you to work with him. No, not right away. That will cause too much pressure. Give it some time, then work with the kid, particularly with his hitting," he continued. "I want you to become his friend. I understand in the minors when he got into a slump, he'd get moody, take off and go home."

"No problem, skip," I immediately replied, feeling the satisfaction as team captain that I would be helping in a leadership role. I understood what Leo wanted and the pitfalls of working with a potentially moody individual. I went over to the batting cage, introduced myself, and then left him alone for about a week. Then I started spending time with Young, principally working on his hitting. I would suggest ways he could alter his stroke, go to the opposite field, regular stuff like that. Additionally, as time wore on, I tried to give him some hints about tendencies of pitchers he would likely be facing.

When the 1969 season started, Young was okay, but not sensational. Frankly, with people like me, Billy Williams, Ernie Banks, Don Kessinger, Glenn Beckert and Randy Hundley as teammates, he didn't have to be the next coming of Willie Mays. His job was to play a solid centerfield, help us defensively and give us an occasional base hit. Which is what he basically did to start the season.

I had been told by scouts that if Young were to struggle at the plate, he would get moody, sullen. Still, he seemed to be working his way through it and seemed generally happy. But by June I noticed he was struggling. His average was down, he was pressing. I had been there before. Every major leaguer, whether he was a Hall-of-Famer or a two-minute wonder, has been there. I took him aside after one particularly tough game. He told me what I probably had figured already. He was down, depressed and thinking of quitting. He was ready to walk away from the Cubs, the major leagues and possibly a chance to be a part of Chicago sports history.

I knew he didn't need an artificial pep talk. I told him the importance of the team, that his role was clearly outlined and he didn't have to exceed to excel. He seemed to accept what I was saying. Or so I thought. A couple of games later, we're involved in a tight game against the Mets. I already had made my comments to Dick Young about the greatness of the Cubs versus the weaknesses of the Mets. Remember, we're still about five or six games in front of both the Cardinals and the oncoming Mets, who I still didn't consider a threat. Plus, we have our ace, Ferguson Jenkins, on the mound.

To appreciate Fergie, you have to look past the statistics. He was involved in so many close games for us I couldn't even begin to speculate on how many additional games he could have won in his career with the Cubs. It's easy to say major league pitchers hate Wrigley Field and can't make it there. But look at Fergie, and it's a completely different story. Hall-of-Famer? You bet. Among the most underrated of all time? Without question. Fergie always knew what he was doing on the mound: where he was going to throw the next pitch, the batters' strengths and weaknesses.

So he likes to position his infield and outfield. The previous inning, we had runners on first and third with a chance to break the game open. But Young hits into an inning-ending double play, snuffing out the rally. Double plays are a part of baseball.

Sometimes, you can hit a rocket that winds up in two outs; other times, you can hit a soft dribbler that will clear the bases. As a veteran, I knew this. Young didn't.

We took the field in the eighth. As the inning began, Jenkins motioned to Young to move in a couple of steps and over a few more. In a cozy park like Wrigley Field, it can mean the difference between a routine pop out and disaster. At

Shea, it might not have been that close a fit but still important.

Only Young wasn't paying any attention to him. Fergie called me over to the mound and asked, "What's with this guy? Get him to move over."

I tried with less success than Jenkins. Jim Hickman tried yelling over to Young to do the same thing, but Young didn't move.

After the inning, Hickman called me over in the dugout.

"You better have a talk with him, Ron. He isn't paying attention to anyone," said Hickman, probably one of the most soft-spoken guys on the team.

I walked over toward Young and took him underneath the dugout to a small hallway leading to the clubhouse. "You okay?" I asked.

"I'm not hitting; I'm in a slump," Young replied.

"Donny, don't worry about it. We're in first place, we've got a five-game lead. You just go out there and play the game. We've got the guys who can do the hitting on this club. Don't worry so much." I could see he was down but he seemed to listen.

Now came the ninth with a two-run lead, and Fergie was still looking great. The lead-off man, Ken Boswell, popped a fly to center that dropped right in front of Young. It should have been caught but it was evident he didn't see it coming off the bat. It was a packed Shea Stadium crowd, and he could have lost it in the shirtsleeves.

Jenkins got a little uptight because he thought he had out number one. However, the next guy went out, and we were two outs away from a victory.

Jenkins was positioning Young over to where he wanted him in left center instead of straight-away center. Jenkins knew that pinch-hitter Donn Clendennon's strengths were to the power alleys. Again, Young didn't budge.

Fergie called me over from third. "What's with this

guy? Why isn't Young moving ?"

I'll move him," I said, motioning to Young from the pitcher's mound. As I motioned, Leo trotted to the mound to see what was happening.

"What the hell is going on out here?" Leo barked.

"Get him to move," Jenkins yelled back.

Leo turned to me, instructing me to get Young in line and right now. "Get his ass over there," Leo retorted, departing for the dugout.

Young saw me motion for him to move to the left. He finally took a couple of steps, but Fergie wanted more. Again, I waved, and again, he was stationary. Finally, Young took a few more steps, and at last, we're set to face Clendennon.

Clendennon lined a ball 10 feet to the right of Young. The ball hit the kid's glove and bounced away. The tying run was now at first, the winning run was at the plate.

Cleon Jones, the best hitter on the Mets, came through and doubled, scoring Boswell and Clendennon, making it 3-3. We decided to walk left-handed hitter Art Shamsky to get the force-out at third base.

Jenkins got Wayne Garrett, a light-hitting infielder, for the second out but the runners advanced. I thought, "At least if we get the last out we can go to extra innings."

But then Ed Kranepool, a member of the original New York Mets, stepped up and cued a wounded duck over my head into left field. Jones scored, the Mets won, and we walked off the field in defeat. Little did I know the subsequent consequences would eventually affect my life.

After the game, I was downcast but Jenkins was uncharacteristically upset. I had never seen him quite like this, particularly because he was so low key. We all trekked into the clubhouse and silently headed toward our individual lockers. I sat down in front of my locker, noticing that Young was visibly upset. I saw him tear his uniform off quickly, bypass taking a shower, dress immediately and begin to leave without talking to the media. I thought this was wrong because he would have to face them eventually.

"Donny, where are you going?" I asked him.

"I'm out of here," Young replied, heading out the back door.

"Listen, Donny, there are a lot of media out there. Sit down, wait for them to come in and then you can leave," I pleaded, remembering Leo's spring training charge to me to watch over the kid. But he was clearly in a terrible mood and he wouldn't listen to me.

In the past, the writers could follow us in immediately, but under the new league rules, we had a 10-minute cooling off period, something that still is in effect to this day. So the writers charged in and as they usually did, headed toward the manager's office. I feared Young would bolt when he saw the group head toward Leo's office but I was wrong. He stayed in front of his locker.

Both the New York and Chicago writers followed custom and heard Leo bark, "My two-year-old could have caught those two f——ing balls!" referring to the Boswell and Clendennon singles.

It was a comment that rang out through our silent clubhouse. Young heard it and he was history that day. He tore off without saying a word to anyone.

My roommate, Glenn Beckert, and I were going to have dinner that night with our wives in New York, so we hung around and had a couple of beers. As I was coming out of the shower, Dick Young of the *Daily News* and Jerome Holtzman of the *Chicago Sun-Times* were waiting for me at my locker. I was surprised they had waited so long after the game to talk to me because I wasn't a key player in that ninth inning. The first question to me was—"What happened out there?"

I knew they were fishing for more information about Young.

"It's like anybody as a rookie. Sometimes you put your

head between your legs. I've done it as a player. Those things happen," I told both writers. At no time did I give the impression, let alone a direct quote, that Don Young cost us the ballgame.

To this day, I swear that is all I said.

I went to the hotel, joined my wife Judy, had some drinks and met the Beckerts for some dinner at the Waldorf Astoria. After dinner at the bar, Judy and I saw veteran *Sun-Times* writer Jack Griffin, one of the top baseball writers ever to write in Chicago. He asked the same question Holtzman did, but I went into further detail, describing Jenkins's futile attempts to get Young in position. I didn't detail the language or say Young had cost us the game but I did discuss the role Leo and the Cubs expected Young to play with the 1969 club.

Judy and I went up to our room, clicked off the lights and went to sleep. At 4:00 A.M., the phone rang. I was startled, naturally, and checked the hotel clock to see if I had overslept. I hadn't. On the other end was a reporter from the CBS station in Chicago.

"Have you any comment?" the reporter asked.

"Comment about what?" I grumbled, trying to wipe away the sleep from my brain.

"The *story*," the reporter insisted.

I didn't know what he was talking about. Athletes will some times say that to avoid commenting on something they don't want to talk about. But in this case, it was sincere.

It was later explained that the *Sun-Times* had done a World War III type headline saying to the effect, "Santo Says Young Loses Game."

I couldn't believe it. I had nothing to say to the reporter. Judy turned over and asked what was wrong. I wasn't sure. I went back to sleep.

At 8:00 A.M., I got another call. Pete Reiser, the former Dodger who was our third base coach, had an immediate order for me.

"Ron, you better get down to Don Young's room immediately because he's packing and getting ready to leave," Reiser explained. "He's had calls from friends in Chicago telling him that you said he lost the game."

I immediately dressed and headed down the hall and knocked on the door of his room.

He opened the door, saw that it was me, didn't shut the door but walked away without closing it. I walked in and shut the door.

"What's the problem?"

"How could you tell the writers that I lost the game?" Young queried.

"Donny, I didn't do it," I told him. " And how could you think that considering all that I have done for you? I'm your biggest booster! I know you've been struggling and as captain of this team, I would never say that any single individual could cost us a game. If you buy this because some friends read the paper and told you, I will call a meeting before the game and apologize to you in front of all the players."

Young seemed settled. He unpacked and we both made plans to head to the ballpark.

When I arrived at the park that afternoon, I went into Leo's office and explained my plan. It was not because I believed I had done anything wrong; I hadn't. I was angry, hurt. But I was the captain of a team in contention for a pennant on a club that had not won anything.

After calling the players together—coaches and Leo were excluded—I made my stand.

"If I said anything to a reporter that could have been misconstrued as criticism, I'm sorry."

Simple and to the point. It was a difficult thing for a proud Italian like myself to do. Still, I thought the matter was behind me.

So I thought.

When we went out to take batting and fielding practice,

about a dozen players came up to me individually. "What did you do?" was the chorus. They had no idea.

Young was out of the lineup for the final two games of the series. We lost to the Mets and Tom Seaver 4-3 but salvaged the final game of the three-game series behind Bill Hands. We had stopped a five-game losing streak and were still in first place.

We arrived back in Chicago, still in first place; it was the middle of the summer and we had a home doubleheader against the Philadelphia Phillies. This deep into my career I'm used to the cheers and adulation we get from the hometown fans. In fact, I had never been booed in my life.

But when I walked on to the field to start the game, I was booed. First, just a few jeers then a larger and larger sound. I was hurt. It was traumatic. My heart sank. This was the team I loved, the ballpark I loved and the fans I loved. We were in first place. And they were booing me over a misunderstanding.

I shook off the disappointment and had a good doubleheader. We won both games and seemed to be back on track. Again, I thought the hits had turned the boos to cheers and the incident was a blip on what I had hoped would be a storybook season for the Cubs.

The very next day, Griffin wrote a column saying I was a villain. Here we go again.

I was shocked that Griffin, who I really admired, would turn on me. After that column, the hate mail began coming to the ballpark with my name on it. Terrible, vindictive stuff. The kind of angst you wouldn't think decent people were capable of saying and doing. Beckert and Gene Oliver would eventually stop me from reading my mail.

Oliver and I became very close pals during the 1969 season and are still close to this day; he was the prankster, the guy who would keep things loose in the clubhouse. He was also an effective pinch hitter for us.

After the Young incident, Oliver decided he would loosen me up. One day before a game in August at Wrigley Field, I came into the clubhouse and saw the stack of mail waiting for me. I always sat down to read the mail, good and bad. Sometimes I would also have baseballs sent to me to be autographed and returned.

As I'm going through my daily ritual, Oliver strolled over to the vicinity of my locker and I overhear him say to Billy Williams, "What's that ticking noise?" Oliver asked.

"Yea, what is that ticking?" Beckert chimed in.

All of a sudden, Billy turns to me.

"Say, Ron, do you hear that ticking?" Williams asked.

I couldn't tell what they were talking about and besides, I was engrossed in this horrendous mail I was receiving.

More of my teammates came over and asked the same question about the ticking.

I finally noticed that a box is in front of me, and it was addressed to me. I picked it up and heard this ticking. I grabbed the box and ran out the clubhouse door, out into left field and threw the box. I then jumped back inside the safety of the clubhouse.

Nothing happened. No explosion, no loud bang, not even a whimper.

I came back in the clubhouse, and my teammates were laughing so hard they were almost on the floor.

"You rotten bastards," I said as I started to laugh. They brought back the box, and I opened it up; it was an egg timer. I realized that the self-torture I was putting myself through was simply paranoia. I had to overcome it.

Little did I know how much more serious things would get. After the conclusion of the season, things took a more ominous turn.

I received a letter on a Tuesday, threatening me, my wife and my children. Crank letters are a part of fame, I suppose. But like the booing, any performer who tells you it doesn't bother or scare him is lying.

What was particularly unnerving was this crackpot knew my routine and my children's as well. He knew when they went to school and where they went to school. It wasn't a formal letter; it was the type of note you'd see from a kidnapper. Strips of paper giving me his message.

I wasn't sure whether this was an off-shoot of the Don Young thing or not. But his threats were real. "How could you do this to a rookie? I'll get even with you," the first letter would say.

I didn't take any chances. I reported it to the club and to the commissioner's office. The following Tuesday, another letter, filled with the same venom, arrived. It would be known cryptically in the Santo household as the "Tuesday letter."

John Holland, the team's general manager, urged me to get police protection. This wasn't a movie; this was real life, he told me. So after the disappointment of 1969, I had to have round-the-clock, 24-hour police protection for some nut who was threatening my family. The media wasn't aware; few outside our family were aware how potentially serious things were at the time.

The letters continued to come but the sender never did. It was a hellish off-season for my family. And then as we prepared for spring training in 1970, the Tuesday letter came as usual. The tone was different.

"I'm sorry for the trouble that I have caused you. I'd like to meet you, alone, at Wrigley Field, at 10:00 P.M. to formally apologize."

When I showed that letter to the police, they stated it simply: "Don't go to that meeting."

Instead, the police had someone drive a Cadillac similar to mine to Wrigley Field. No one came. For a brief period, I thought this adventure was over.

However, the next week, the Tuesday letter came.

"You lied to me. You didn't show up."

The chill went through my entire body. But it would be the last time I would receive the Tuesday letter.

At the end of the 1970 season, we were winding up the campaign with a week-long road trip. In Montreal, Holland and Leo called me into their office after the game and sat me down. Instinctively, I believed it was a pep talk. I was wrong.

"Ron, we got a couple of calls at Wrigley," Leo said. The atmosphere in the room was tense. Was I being dealt? I was aware Leo had tried to trade me in the past and maybe this was it.

But judging from the expressions from Holland and Durocher I knew it wasn't baseball-related. In a split second, I started to wonder if something had happened to my kids or my wife.

"Ron, we got a couple of calls into the switchboard at Wrigley Field. Plus, we've received a letter threatening your life. We have to inform you of this. Now, it happens a lot to some guys on contending teams. They're usually cranks, but we feel it best to inform you," Holland said.

I had heard of this before but not to a member of the Cubs or to me.

John, what is the concern here?" I asked, probably still in shock from the threat.

"Ron, there's been a threat on your life. It's not one call, it's several calls. We've called the commissioner's office and we want to give you security going into Philadelphia and New York."

Security? What the hell was going on?!

Holland explained the threat was that someone would shoot from me from the stands. No more information than that.

I wasn't thinking that this was an outgrowth of the Tuesday letter. The caller had stated a specific city (New York), a specific game (a day game) and a specific time

(2:00 P.M.). I was trying to rationalize what was happening and also, partly as a defense mechanism, attempting to downplay it.

"John, doesn't this crap happen all of the time?" I asked.

"Yes, but we feel that with the calls and letters it would be better to have some officers greet you once you get off the plane in Philadelphia and stay with you," Holland instructed. "I want you to go straight to the hotel room once the game is over and stay there. They'll be there with you."

"You mean these guys are staying and following me?" I asked incredulously. This can't all be happening. It's too Hollywood I thought.

"We want protection because Philly is so close to New York," Holland said.

I got on that plane from Montreal, and we headed toward Philadelphia, where two big bruising-looking guys greet me as the team deplanes. My teammates were not aware of the threat or the protection measures the commissioner's office and the Cubs had worked out. Beckert, my long-time roommate on the road, sensed something wasn't right. I confided in him the story of the threats, knowing I would be able to trust him.

During the Philly series, these guys were with me all of the time: On the bus, at the hotel, at Veterans Stadium. It took about 24 hours for the word to get around the team that something was up with me. The reaction was part macabre, part humorous. Some of the guys thought it was a joke and pulled a few stunts. Looking back, it may have reduced the tension.

When we arrived in New York for the final series (and I was hoping "final" meant last of the year) security had become even tighter. The two security guys were stationed in the room next to mine, although I can't say it made it any easier to sleep. They rode the freight elevators with me to and from the room; the regular elevators were off limits.

Beckert, a fun-loving guy, the kind of player you would want for your brother, knew what this was doing to me and had a plan. My dear roomie placed a large sign on his bed: "Glenn Beckert sleeps here." He didn't want to have any cases of mistaken identity.

The next morning I woke up and noticed Beckert was gone already. The bus wasn't going to leave for Shea Stadium until 11:00 A.M. and it's only 10:00 A.M. Why was Beckert out of the room so early?

The phone rang and I picked it up. "You've got one hour and you're gone."

I immediately called our FBI friends next door and relayed the conversation.

"Stay right here, we're going to be watching," they said. It wasn't the kind of comforting I was looking for at that moment.

Moments later, I heard a knock on the door. Naturally, hindsight is 20-20. If someone is going to kill you, they're not going to come to a crowded hotel, knock on the door, wipe their feet and rub you out. But I'm not thinking that rationally.

I heard some rumbling outside the door. The security guys had pinned someone to the wall. I looked outside. It was Phil Regan, the Vulture, our relief ace. Phil didn't think all of these death threats were that serious. I had to laugh, albeit nervously, at the site of these two bruisers smearing Phil against the wall.

When we finally got to Shea Stadium, there was a light rain so we didn't take batting practice, just some light fielding practice before the game. As I was dressing, Beckert came over to me.

"Say, Ron, let's give Paul Popovich (one of our utility infielders) your number 10 today. He'll take infield practice for you, and if they are really out to get you, they'll shoot Popovich instead," Beckert said with a straight face.

Obviously, my roommate wasn't taking any of this melodrama too seriously. I kept my number 10, skipped infield practice and sat in front of my locker as I had been instructed to do.

As I was about to make the walk to the dugout, the two security guys and Holland walked in and approach me. "Ron, come into Leo's office, will you?" Holland asked.

By now, I was fairly weary of these meetings in Leo's office.

"Ron, the security wires at Shea Stadium have been cut," Holland announced. Was this Beckert's latest attempt at a gag or was this the real thing? I wondered. Holland continued. "We don't know if this is connected to the threats."

I was as nervous as I've been in my life. "We're going to put you on a plane to Chicago with the security force and you're going home," Holland concluded, leaving no doubt he didn't want any debate on the subject. "We'll pack your bags and send them. We'll have an officer to take you home."

There was a part of me that wanted to balk at the idea of leaving my team and my job before work was over. There was another part of me that was concerned about the safety and welfare of my family. But I was a family man first, company man second.

A plane was waiting for me at La Guardia. I had a first class ticket, and I was the only one sitting in first class, which was unsettling to me. We were supposed to take off on time but then there was a delay. First 10 minutes, then 20 minutes. By now, I was having a complete conversation with myself. "What the hell is going on?" was the crux of the dialogue. "This guy who is out to get me has to know I'm on this plane."

After about a 30 minute delay, which seemed like an eternity, a guy walked into the plane with a little black bag. My eyes focused on that bag, not the guy's face. I was sitting alone, remember, in first class, on an aisle seat. The guy had the pick of any window seat he wanted among the 12 or so empty seats. He sat next to me across the aisle.

My mind was racing. James Bond scenarios came into focus. All I can see is this black bag filled with the weapons of death. I'm forming a game plan: When the plane began to taxi and the engines were roaring, I was convinced he was going for the black bag. But before he got a hand on it, I'd be going for his jaw.

We finally got ready to take off. There was still no movement from this guy.

The first class stewardess, unaware of my Agatha Christie mindset, walked over to me with a broad smile. "Anything to drink, sir?" she asked.

"Double scotch." Two words were all I could utter.

The scotch came. I sipped it, alternating glances between the black bag and my ice cubes. After a period of time, I had to go to the john. But as I returned, I realized the guy wasn't there. The bag was, he wasn't. I figured he would trigger this bomb or whatever during the landing when the engines are roaring. I was giving him a lot of credit for a master plan. Now I was sure the guy was in the other john so I was going to take a peek into the black bag, but before I got a chance to inspect the contents, he emerged from the other lavatory.

We made the approach toward O'Hare. The pilot was pointing out great Chicago landmarks, but believe me, the Water Tower, Lake Michigan and Wrigley Field were of little concern. My eyes were on the bag. If this guy has any plans for me, I thought, I'm ready for him. But we landed without incident. A police officer came aboard and escorted me off the plane and then home.

The black bag and the man vanished.

Were the Shea Stadium threats related to the Tuesday letters? To this day I don't think so. As for the man with the black bag, I suppose he was the product of some well-deserved paranoia.

The investigation into the Tuesday letters concluded that this guy was in love with me, and my failure to respond to his letters was being taken as romantic rejection. Then the letters suddenly stopped. The security escorting my kids eventually was stopped as was the round-the-clock protection. For more than a year, my family and I had visited hell. It was finally over.

But the "Don Young" incident never went away. To this day it haunts me, and fans and critics alike associate it with me and remember 1969 more for that than for all of the wonderful things that would happen to us in that season.

A footnote: Young's only season with us was in 1969. He was out of baseball a short time after that. I subsequently saw Young again at one of Randy Hundley's fantasy camps in the early '80s. We said hello to one another, talked for a bit and that was it. Many people think we have animosity between one another; that's not true. The one lingering disappointment I have is that Young never came out publicly to say it wasn't my fault.

nine

Ron Santo Day

I'm not sure whether we should have been favored to win it all in 1970. I know personally I was just about as confident about our chances that year as I was the previous year. But it didn't come to pass for us in 1970. It may have been our last great chance with the club we had to go all the way.

There was some satisfaction that the Mets didn't win it in 1970, either. Those who were predicting a dynasty for the great young Mets of 1969 had to think again. The Pirates, a club I had respected because of Roberto Clemente, won the division that year and at least we did finish ahead of the Mets, albeit in second place.

While we didn't grab the brass ring in 1970, either, I did have the game of my life. And it should have come as no surprise to anyone that it came against my old buddy Gene Mauch and the Expos on July 6.

Big days in the major leagues are part skill, part luck, a lot of opportunity. There are days when the ball seems as big as a beach ball but you hit it right at someone. And there are those days when you hit the hell out of the ball and there's no one on base to drive in.

This day, everything worked right. In the first game, I banged out a two-run homer off Carl Morton, and we won the opener 3-2. Nothing special here. I hit 342 lifetime homers in my career, and this was just one of them.

But in the second game, we were facing Mike Wegener, and in the very first inning, I hit a grand slam, one of five I hit in my career. The next time up, the bases are again loaded, so I have a chance to hit back-to-back grand slams. But they walked me so I've got five RBI in just four innings.

Next time up, they finally got me out. Because it was a doubleheader and there were no lights, the game was going into darkness. In the middle of the summer, we could normally play until around 6:00 P.M. but because we're scoring so much, it's getting near that bewitching hour. So, the umpires suspend the game, and we pick it up the very next afternoon. That was standard procedure throughout my career. We were the only ballpark that faced that dilemma and now with lights at Wrigley, suspended games because of darkness have gone the way of the Edsel. We had played a lot of games late into the day facing the possibility of suspending the game; the umpires always seem to know when to call a game, so I never had to face the prospect of a line drive down my throat and my not seeing it. Twilight was always the most difficult time for hitters on the road; at Wrigley Field, twilight was never a concern. We were showered and out the door by then.

We resumed the next day, and I was the first up for us in the seventh inning. I hit a three-run homer off Claude Raymond, who would later become a French-speaking broadcaster for the Expos, and that made it 14-2 Cubs.

My totals for the day: 3 for 8 with 10 RBI, eight of them coming in the second game alone. On the year, I wound up driving 114 runs but that was only good enough for third on the team. Williams had 129 and Hickman 115. Not many times in baseball history has someone driven in 114 runs and wound up third on his own team.

There was a different atmosphere beginning in 1971, the year that wound up being Leo's last full year with us. The Pirates were the team to beat again and to their credit, they defended their title. We had slipped to third place that year, but now were 14 games off the pace, tied with the Mets. But things were different. Ernie had retired and Randy Hundley and Jim Hickman were gone.

It was also the year that I almost killed Leo. For the most part, I had escaped the wrath of Leo. Until 1971. This was two years after our great run of 1969, and Leo probably knew that our big chance to make it to the World Series had passed him by with the Cubs. We were still in the race in mid-season and then we hit a snag. We lost five in a row heading into a series with the Cincinnati Reds, who were at the embryonic stages of the Big Red Machine.

Leo had called a meeting at the old clubhouse located at the end of the left field stands at Wrigley Field (the club has since moved to better quarters behind the third base dugout). Normally during a meeting, the door was shut for obvious reasons: to keep the press out. On this occasion, he had longtime equipment manager Yosh Kawano lock the door and put a cover over the one window that the media could look in to at this crowded clubhouse. The CIA couldn't penetrate this type of security. We didn't know what to expect, even after six years with Leo.

Durocher came in and stood in the middle of the locker room. He brought along a chair and stood on it. He started out calmly.

"We're not playing good baseball. I get the feeling that something is wrong here," Leo said, almost fatherly. "For some unknown reason, maybe it's me. So, I want you guys to tell me if it's me. If I'm pissing you off, now is the time to let me know. Look on me as if I were a player, not a manager."

It was a setup. And we knew it.

"C'mon, someone has to have a problem on this team," Leo said, trying to encourage us to speak up.

Again, no hands were raised. But out of the corner of my eye, I saw Pepitone's hand shoot up.

"Skip, now, uh, do you, uh, really, uh, mean this?" Pepitone blurted out. He knew it was a setup, too, but he had to take a shot.

"Absolutely, Joe," Leo said, still quiet in his tone and demeanor. The calm before the storm, I wondered?

"Okay, look here. I played for Ralph Houk with the Yankees and he was a players' manager," Pepitone said. Now, on the top 10 list of the things that would light the fuse was saying Leo wasn't a players' manager.

"Lately, Skip, we aren't playing good. But I read in the newspapers where you are criticizing some of us for our mistakes. You never used to do that," Pepitone continued on his own death march.

Leo jumped up. Those infamous veins started bulging. "Now, who the f— do you think you are?! The only f——ing reason you are on this ballclub is ME! You were out of the f——ing game! If it weren't for me, you'd be in the f——ing gutter, you asshole," Leo screamed. The tirade probably lasted about five minutes, although it seemed like five seasons.

The one thing the rest of us could take solace in was that he wasn't screaming at us. Until Leo suddenly turned to me.

"The rest of you f——ers, if you were like Glenn Beckert, who does everything extra, we'd ALL be better off! He comes out early, takes extra batting practice and does the extra things," Leo continued, even though Beckert had not taken extra BP for a couple of weeks.

Leo was looking at me, and as captain, I decided to tread into the waters. "Listen Skip, wait a minute. Beckert isn't the only one who comes here early. A lot of us are doing the same thing; coming early, staying late." Maybe I should have not gotten into it with him, but my Italian blood was starting to rise.

And then Leo said, "Well, the only f——ing reason they're having a Ron Santo Day in this ballpark is because YOU asked for one!"

I went nuts.

"You lying S.O.B.! I never asked for a Ron Santo Day! You get John Holland down here right this instant! You won't embarrass ME in front of MY teammates!"

I grabbed Leo and had him around the neck.

"Go ahead, if you want to, hit me," Leo challenged.

Not only am I a lot bigger and stronger than Leo but I'm half his age. I could have killed him. Jim Hickman and Billy Williams finally pulled us apart. They sat me down, and Leo stormed up to his office without saying another word. I still wanted a piece of him but fortunately, I couldn't break loose from the Hickman-Williams grip. I'm so mad at this point tears are streaming down my face.

A couple of minutes passed, and I then stormed up to Leo's office. No one was going to stop me. I opened his door and slammed it.

"You get John Holland down here right now! You get his ass down here!" I shouted. The sound of pounding fists on Leo's door could be heard. I can't imagine what my teammates were thinking I was going to do.

Holland came hurrying down. Leo wanted to talk to him privately, but I wouldn't allow it. "John, Leo says I begged for a Ron Santo Day. You tell him I didn't ask for this f——ing day," I implored.

Holland turned to me and said, "Ron, don't worry, I'm

going to handle this." I took Holland's advice and went back down to the clubhouse.

Five minutes passed and the two of them came down. "John, you tell my teammates that I didn't ask for this day," I again demanded.

Holland hesitated. That slight hesitation was a signal to me. I turned to Holland. "You bastard."

Holland then turned to the rest of the team. "Fellas, this thing has gotten out of hand. Ron never asked for this day."

Leo, hearing Holland's admission, turned around. "I QUIT!" Leo yelled and again stormed back to his office.

"Let him go," said Kenny Holtzman, one of Leo's leading detractors on the club.

When Holland heard Holtzman, he tried to rally the troops and get control of this potentially explosive situation. "We can't have this guy leave," Holland tried to persuade the team. "We're not out of this race. If we let Leo quit now, the press will bury us. You have to go up there. Ron, you are the captain, go up there and get it settled."

I was still furious. I couldn't understand why Holland hadn't simply told Leo he was wrong about my pushing for a Ron Santo Day and that would be the end of it. I wasn't in a compromising mood.

"We gave you the day, Ron, but I'm in a bind. Help me out," Holland pleaded.

"Let me cool off. I'll do it. If someone wants to go up now, fine, but I need some time."

No one else volunteered to go into the lion's den. After 10 minutes, I did go up to Leo's office. He was already dressed in his street clothes. "Leo, it got out of hand. We both lost our tempers. I wasn't offended, Leo. Let's try to forget it. We're both competitive guys. We need you. If you leave us now, it's going to be bad for everyone." It was partly the diplomat in me that allowed me to say those words through the anger I still felt. He stayed.

Upon reflection, I believe Leo was still upset at Pepitone, not at me. But you couldn't tell that from Leo's book, *Nice Guys Finish Last*, where he took some shots at me from the clubhouse incident and other times.

I think by the time Leo left in the middle of the 1972 season, it was a case of burnout. Our near-miss in 1969 was also a big disappointment to him. When we didn't win it the following year, it was also a big disappointment for him. I'm sure he sensed this might be the last time for him to lead a team into the World Series. When he resigned in 1972 near mid-season and was replaced by Whitey Lockman, I wasn't surprised. I don't think many of us were. You could see all the signs for some time.

I had just figured that Leo, after his salad days with the Brooklyn Dodgers and New York Giants as a young manager, and after his tenure with the glitzy Los Angeles Dodgers and his six-plus stormy seasons with the Chicago Cubs, would just simply go back home and retire.

I was wrong, again, to count out Leo.

By season's end, Leo was back managing again, this time with the Houston Astros. I'm sure he figured he would work the same magic with a second division club near the bottom like Houston that he did with us. He actually started to duplicate his magic in 1973 when he led the Astros to an 82-80 mark, which was five games better than we finished under Whitey Lockman in his first full season with us. But after the 1973 season, Leo had decided to retire. This time, it was for good.

The postscript to our relationship was written in 1982. Many members of the 1969 club had met at one of Randy Hundley's fantasy camps in Arizona. Hundley was the innovator of the fantasy camp idea where everyday people can play right alongside ex-players.

At a closing banquet of that camp, a lot of the members of the 1969 club were there. So was Leo. He got up very slowly to speak. He was a lot older now. What hair he had left was gray, and it was clear he had mellowed from his rough days as our manager.

He got up before the entire group of my teammates and apologized for the incident. He spoke in a soft voice, and it was obvious he was sincere.

The tears were streaming down my face as he talked; there really wasn't a dry eye in the room. We shook hands, embraced, and I think the feud, what was left of it, had come to an end.

Nineteen seventy-one was a solid one for me at the plate: 21 homers, 88 RBI. But the season was memorable for more than statistics. For all of the friction caused by the plans for the Ron Santo Day, it would turn out to be one of the most wonderful experiences in my life.

We were facing the Atlanta Braves on a Saturday afternoon of August 1971. It was also the NBC Game of the Week, back when they had the good sense to show a national game every week of the season. The Cubs flew my stepfather, mother and sister in to see the game. My wife and two children, Linda and Ron, Jr., were there with me on the field. Nearly 35,000 Cub fans were there, all wearing "Ron Santo Day" buttons.

The microphone was set up in front of home plate before the game. Jack Brickhouse, the voice of the Cubs on TV, was the master of ceremonies. I had made it clear that any donations from that day be directed toward Juvenile Diabetes Foundation of Greater Chicago. I had, by then, given the Cubs' organization permission to publicly announce for the first time that I had the disease, even though most of my teammates had been aware for several years.

I probably wasn't prepared for what was going to happen; I didn't request this honor despite what Leo or anyone else might have thought. I had given 11 years of my life to the Cubs, and they saw fit to reward me, and I was deeply moved by the gesture.

They gave my wife a mink coat; they gave me a speedboat and a car. They also gave us an all-expense-paid trip to Italy, although for some reason, I never took that trip. I suppose one of these days I'll have to go over there and seek out my roots. I'm not sure the offer on the all-expenses-paid part is still valid.

My teammates gave me an engraved shotgun. There was some needling, not much. Leo didn't cause a stink.

It was an emotionally draining day for me. I hardly remember going up to the microphone or saying anything. I hadn't prepared a speech. The only thing I remember was my daughter Linda crawling around the ground, pulling on the leg of my uniform.

We went on to play the game versus the Braves; I didn't get a hit. The spectacle of having so many fans cheering for me and my teammates supporting me was probably too much for me on that day.

As much as that was a highlight in 1971, one of the lowlights of my life occurred the next year, 1972.

During spring training, the Beckerts and the Santos had condos right next to each other at Scottsdale. I had all three of my children, Ron, Jr., who was twelve at the time; Jeff, who was ten; and Linda, who was only four, down there with us for a large portion of the time.

I had invited my mother and my stepfather, John Constantino, down to Arizona. They had never been down to spring training before due, in part, I guess, to a fortune teller telling my mom that she would die in a plane crash.

My stepfather worked for Boeing in Seattle, the largest employer in the city, but that did little to alleviate my mother's concerns about flying. John liked to drive, anyway; he was slow and careful.

One week before we broke camp in late March, my

mom called to tell me they were packing the car and wouldn't rush down to Arizona. They would enjoy the scenery and take their time; other than to see me in Chicago, she really hadn't ventured much out of the Seattle area.

She told me they would probably get to Phoenix by late Sunday. I said that was fine, knowing that it would normally be a quick two-day trip but they would stretch it out over the entire weekend.

On Sunday morning, the phone rang. I glanced at the clock and saw it was 3:00 A.M. Instinctively, I felt something was wrong and wouldn't answer the phone. I asked Judy to pick it up.

My sister, Adielene, was on the other end. I could see Judy's face. I grabbed the phone and heard Ad tell me my parents had been killed in an automobile accident.

I was in shock. I tried to get some sketchy details about the accident and managed to tell my sister I would call her back.

Judy called Beckert and asked him to come over with his wife, Mary. We had to make the plans for the funeral back in Seattle.

As dawn came, the reality of the tragedy began to set in. Beckert took care of informing my teammates and management. I flew the family up to Seattle the next day and Beckert insisted on coming with me for support; I told him it wasn't necessary, he had done more than any friend could ask.

As we arrived at the Phoenix airport, I was about to load my family on to the plane when I see Beckert walking toward us. "I'm coming with you," Beckert said in a firm tone.

I took a deep breath and hugged him; he helped me keep a clear head throughout this terrible time.

I decided on a Catholic funeral; I had been raised as a Catholic and my stepfather was Catholic. My mother was not. The first priest I approached in my neighborhood refused to preside over the mass because my mother was not a Catholic.

My first real major league fight, in 1962 versus the Reds and Bob Purkey.

Billy and I meeting with Phil Wrigley, Jr., son of Cubs owner P.K. Wrigley.

Lou Boudreau, the man who brought me to the majors.

Hospitalized after the beaning by Jack Fisher. The hitting streak was more alive than I felt at that moment.

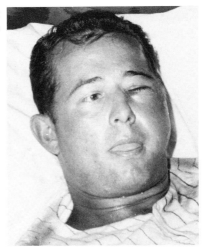

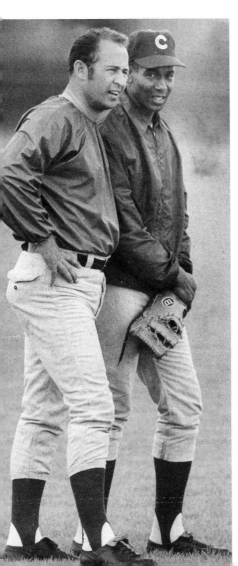

Ernie and I talking over the prospects for 1968 on a cool day at spring training.

A heroic swing for
a homer off the
Reds' Mel Queen.

My sixth Gold Glove, with my roommate, Glenn Beckert, in 1968.

You see, Leo and I really did get along—most of the time.

Doin' the limbo to get away from a pitch from Atlanta's Ron Reed.

High-fiving Jim Hickman's head after a key homer, June, 1969.

A small step for mankind, a near miss for the 1969 Cubs.

One of my 342 round-trippers, April, 1970.

Ron Santo Day, 1971. Linda Santo gives her dad some hitting pointers.

A quick dental checkup
after a ground ball ate
me up against the Expos.

Tommy Lasorda in the middle as umpire Jerry Dale and I go at it.

The Santo clan on Ron Santo Day: stepdad John, sister Adeline, Mom, Linda, Ron Jr. and Jeff.

Thanks to the fans.

(opposite) Clicking my heels.

Thom Brennaman, Bob Brenly and I: the 1990 Cubs broadcast team.

Before I was traded, before
he was (almost) impeached.

Ernie, Billy and I going into the Cubs Walk of Fame.

Jim Frey, Harry Caray and I going over strategy on the field and for the broadcast booth.

The Santos: Jeff, Ron Jr., Linda, Ron Sr., Vicki and Kelly.

Photographs courtesy of the Chicago Tribune.

I was upset, until I found a priest who would preside.

It took about four days to take care of family business, and Beckert and I returned for the start of the season.

I had developed the habit throughout my career of picking up the phone and calling my mother every other day. We would talk about the previous days' games; she would critique what I was doing on the field and at the plate. She would constantly check out the top 10 hitters in the league and would often chide the newspapers for being a point or two off in my current correct batting average.

Early in my career, before she learned the particulars of the box score, I called her after a particularly poor day in the field.

"Ron, I'm checking out this box score but I have a question. Is there another Santo that played in that game?" she asked.

"Mom, I'm the only Santo in baseball today, believe me," I answered.

"Well, then who is this E. Santo?" she asked in a serious tone.

She would eventually learn that "e" stood for "error" and on occasion, that other phantom Santo, E. Santo, would get into the box score.

During the season after her death, I would reach for the phone to make that call. It took me a long time to get over that sudden tragedy.

The season didn't get much better for me. I suffered a debilitating injury that knocked me out for weeks, and all because I broke one of my cardinal rules: don't fraternize with enemy players during the season; there are rules on this subject, and I'm sure there is a reason for them. It's better that you don't know the guy you are going to face on a particular day; that's just my opinion.

On our first trip into Houston, Jimmy Stewart, who had been our teammate and was now a utility infielder with the Astros, called me up on our off day.

"Say, Ron, want to get in a game of golf on our day off?" Stewart asked.

"Sure. I'll bring along someone from the team, and we'll make it a threesome," I suggested.

I arrived at the course and found Stewart, a notorious practical joker and agitator. I also found he had brought along Larry Dierker, the ace right-handed pitcher of the Astros. I had nothing against Dierker, but Stewart, having been a former teammate, knew I was dead set against fraternizing with another team's pitcher.

I was upset and let Stewart know about it. Yet, here we were, ready to tee off, and I suppose I didn't want to act like a baby and walk off. So Stewart, Dierker, Glenn Beckert and myself played the round, and Stewart suggested we go out and have some dinner and a few drinks.

Again, I scoffed at the suggestion; I didn't want to be talking with Dierker about baseball or anything before a game. Stewart knew that but still brought Dierker along. What I really had feared was that Dierker, who I used to hit pretty well, would eventually ask me why I was so successful against him.

The evening wore on and it was pleasant enough until, as I had predicted, Dierker brought up the subject that I had feared.

"Say, Ron, why is it that you always hit me so well?" Dierker asked predictably. "What is your secret?"

I tried to be diplomatic. "Just lucky, I guess. Got to go. See you later, Larry."

I did not forget that incident when Houston made its first trip into Wrigley Field. The Astros, like the Mets, had come into the league as an expansion team in 1962. But unlike the Mets, the Astros had continued to flounder and never grabbed the brass ring the way New York had in that infamous 1969 season. In fact, the Astros are still waiting to get into their first World Series in 1993 while the Mets have made three trips to the Fall Classic.

In the first game of the series, Houston, which was playing good ball and would wind up second that year in their division behind the Big Red Machine, sent Dierker to the mound. And in my first at-bat, Dierker whistled a fastball toward my face. Was it deliberate? Was it part of the aftermath of our golf-dinner evening? That's why I didn't like to socialize with pitchers; you don't want to know what they are thinking when something like that happens.

I didn't have time to think about that; instinctually, I held my wrist up to guard my face. Thousands of ballplayers do the same thing when they think they are going to get hit in the head. And sure enough, the ball hit my wrist, not my face. It stung for a moment, but I shook it off and headed toward first. I glared into the Astros' dugout, looking for Stewart as if to say, "That's why I didn't want you to bring a pitcher along."

We didn't score that inning, and I came back to our dugout, grabbed my glove and headed out to third.

It wasn't until my next at-bat that I sensed something was wrong, dreadfully wrong. I couldn't grasp the bat. My wrist was throbbing now. They took me to Northwestern Memorial Hospital for the usual x-rays; I assumed it was being done as a precaution. But then Dr. Suker arrived and gave me the bad news.

"Ron, it's broken. We're going to have to put it in a cast," he said.

"Cast!? What do you mean, cast? I'm not going to be able to play tomorrow?"

"Ron, you're not going to be able to play for three, four, maybe five weeks." Five weeks? All from getting hit by a guy who I had owned and who I didn't even want to talk to but got trapped into a foursome with that rotten Jimmy Stewart!?

I accepted my fate reluctantly, much the same as I had when I got beaned in the face and couldn't see.

I headed back to my house in Glenview and turned on the television. The game was over and Dierker won. He was interviewed by Jack Brickhouse on the "Tenth Inning" postgame show and Brickhouse, knowing of my success against Dierker, asks the obvious question.

"Was that a purpose pitch you threw at Santo?" Brickhouse queries.

"Oh no, not at all," Dierker chuckled. "Ron and I are good friends. We played golf when he was in Houston."

I wanted to get a gun and shoot that television right in the heart.

I wound up missing 29 games that season because of the injury, the most I would ever miss in a single season in a Cubs' uniform. But I didn't go on the disabled list, and I still hit .302 with 17 homers and 74 RBI. I never went on the disabled list in my career, something I am proud of to this day and something few ballplayers of today can say about their career.

Nineteen seventy-two was also the year Leo called it quits in the middle of the season. And considering the love-hate relationship we had, I had mixed feelings. Leo did bring us respect, something woefully lacking for the Chicago Cubs. He brought us closer to a pennant than anyone else had in a generation. But he also brought disruption and chaos; anyone who was in that turbulent clubhouse mess that brought us to near blows could support that.

When he first came with the club, we were in awe because of his reputation. But the pressures started getting to him after the 1969 failure. It was clear on his face, in his actions and in his demeanor. I'm sure we took the cue from him. I'm not saying our descent in the early 1970s was Leo's fault; we were probably all in a prolonged hangover from the disappointment of that season.

In 1971, we were still playing over .500, but the cracks were beginning to show. Ernie was gone and to paraphrase

Lloyd Bentsen, Joe Pepitone was no Ernie Banks. We had Johnny Callison and Hickman sharing time in the outfield, and they were well into their 30s. The rest of the infield was still intact, but we weren't the young mavericks we were back in '67.

Fergie was still magnificent; he won 24 games that year and Milt Pappas, robbed of that perfect game, won 17. But it was a steep drop after that, and our bullpen was on the decline.

Halfway into the 1972 season, we were a 44-42 club; not out of the race and not half-bad but not a serious contender. The direction was different, and then Leo quit.

Whitey Lockman took over, and he actually did better than Leo (39-26) and we finished second. But it was a distant second, 11 games behind the Pittsburgh Pirates.

I knew that 1971 and 1972 were our last gasps. On paper, we were still a first division team the next three years, but I knew we were on a downward spiral. We had a lot of enthusiasm under Whitey Lockman, but the atmosphere was much different than our peak years with Leo. The club was getting older; Billy was 35, Hickman was 36, I was 33 and Beckert was 32.

The front office realized what we knew. I'm sure they wanted to stay with the veteran lineup the first two years after 1969, but 1972 was the last shot. When Leo left, it was clear they were going to bring up the back of the truck. The old gang didn't disappear in one fell swoop; it was piece-by-piece.

In 1973, Beckert was hurt for part of the year. I came back from my wrist injury with 20 homers and 67 RBI, decent numbers but not what I had been putting up. Two newcomers, centerfielder Rick Monday and pitcher Rick Reuschel, had decent years, but we fell below .500 for the first time since the debacle of 1966 at 77-84.

It was a strange year. The hated Mets seemed to come out of nowhere to be in first place in September. The Cardinals, who had something like an 8-28 record at one point, had been in first on Labor Day but were slumping. The defending division champion Pirates were hovering around .500 as were the young Expos. Strange as it seemed, we weren't playing good baseball and we were only a half dozen games out. But it's one thing to be six games or so out in September and be in second place, 20 games over .500. It's quite another thing to be six games out, in fourth place, seven or eight games below .500.

The race did come down to the final week of the season. The Mets owned a one-game lead over the Cardinals and had to come to Wrigley Field to play us in a makeup doubleheader the day after the regular season ended. If we swept the doubleheader, there would have been a tie between the Cardinals and the Mets. Talk about a tough decision for Cub fans; our two arch-rivals. I wanted to go out and play the doubleheader hard no matter whom we were playing. But I suppose I wanted to do all I could to see that the Mets didn't win it, particularly in our ballpark.

The Mets beat us in the first game of the doubleheader before only a couple of thousand soul-hearty fans on a lousy day. The second game was canceled because mathematically, the race was over and New York was in the playoffs, and we were headed for winter vacation. Again, the Mets prevailed in the playoffs but at least this time, they didn't grab the World Series. The Oakland A's took care of that.

I didn't realize at that time it would be the last game I would play in a Chicago Cubs' uniform. I sensed changes were coming; I didn't know they would involve me. But hindsight is 20-20. The front office had waited too long to make the changes necessary to infuse strong young players as a way to gradually replace the veterans. Instead, they went too long with the veterans, including me, probably, and the team fell apart.

Also, the farm system was poor and wasn't producing the kind of players to replace the veterans. This has been a nagging problem for the Cubs over the past 30 years. Remember Gene Lawing, the scout who didn't want to sign me? He was only 5'8", and it seemed that for several years, he wouldn't recommend signing anyone over 6'. You can imagine how that compared to other clubs who were left to get all of the hundreds of prospects over that diminutive level. That didn't help build the Cubs' farm system.

Many suggest the Wrigley family was too cheap; that just wasn't the case, plain and simple. Our 1969 club, for example, was well paid, considering the times. We had veterans that were earning more than the average salary for major league players at the time.

It isn't always about spending money. Look at the current ownership, the Tribune Company, who certainly has been willing to commit funds to make this organization a winner. The team is still beset by problems in the farm system; the *Sporting News* ranked it at the bottom of the major leagues for the 1992 season. So, money can't always buy you out of your problems.

Digression about third basemen: Many have suggested the Cubs haven't had a regular strong third baseman since that time. Bill Madlock and Ron Cey put together two or three good seasons in a row. But I was their third baseman for nearly 15 years, and in 1993, the Cubs are going on yet another third baseman in Steve Buechele that they hope will finally settle down the position.

Third base may be the Rodney Dangerfield position in baseball over the last 30 years. When I played, there were some truly outstanding ones: Eddie Mathews, Ken Boyer, Brooks Robinson. But only seven third basemen are in the Hall of Fame. That's the fewest at any position in all of baseball.

Today, you can look toward Wade Boggs and possibly Terry Pendleton as third basemen who have done the job over a period of years. Pendleton has had two great back-to-back seasons for Atlanta in 1991 and 1992, but it remains to be seen whether he can do it over a long period of time.

The Cubs have been searching for a regular third baseman to anchor that spot much the way Ryne Sandberg—who originally came up as a third baseman—has done at second for them for the past decade. But most other major league clubs are also looking for a veteran third baseman who will cement the infield and be there for a solid 10 years.

I can't say definitively why there aren't more third basemen in Cooperstown or why there always seems to be a need for talent at that position. It is a very difficult position to play; good young players don't like playing it. Maybe the strain of playing third takes away from the mental concentration that is needed to be a potent force offensively. Youngsters with good athletic ability are usually put at shortstop or pitcher because they have good arms. They aren't put at third base.

Third base requires the best reflexes on a team. Maybe the reflex action is more difficult to scout in young players; maybe others are afraid of having the ball slammed down their throat playing so close to the batter's box. After all, a majority of hitters are right-handed rather than left-handed so it's the third baseman, rather than the first baseman, who is looking down the barrel of the gun. Maybe it's so the first baseman can have a little company when he is holding a runner on base.

Another requirement is concentration. The third baseman probably has to concentrate more than any other position in the field; a pitcher who is predominantly a fastball pitcher means you are going to get a lot of balls pulled your way. You will need a strong chest to knock down those line drives; you will also need a strong head to stay in the game. If you have fear, you are going to be doomed. Fear has driven more potentially good young third basemen out of that position. And yes, you have to be a good athlete, and in my mind, third basemen are better athletes than pitchers.

So there I was in 1973, still pounding away at third, and proud of it. I planned to spend the rest of my career there. I always imagined I would play my entire career with the team, get a gold watch and then retire into private business. I had heard rumors of trades involving myself throughout my career: the one Leo mentioned when he was coaching with the Dodgers, and the one Leo tried to make when he was manager of the Cubs. He tried to make a deal before 1969 to send me to the Minnesota Twins that fell through. The hot stove league in the winter would always bring my name up, particularly after our near-miss in 1969.

But each spring, there I was, ready to pack to go to Mesa, Arizona, for another spring training. As much as I knew the Cubs were in for an overhaul, I didn't think part of that process would involve me.

I was wrong.

ten

Billy, Ernie, Fergie and I

I make no pretense about my place in Cub history. I was a player who had to make the most of his ability; whatever tools God gave me I had to utilize to be the best that I could. I consider myself to have been gifted with outstanding athletic abilities; I wanted to make sure I was never content with just getting by.

In my era with the Cubs, there were four clearly dominant personalities with the team. Their impact is still being felt today.

Ernie Banks and Billy Williams were clearly the two best hitters I ever played with. Ferguson Jenkins was the best pitcher on our club. The three of them dominated the National League in the '60s and early '70s. That's why they are in the Hall of Fame in Cooperstown.

And then there was Philip K. Wrigley, owner of the Cubs, heading up the Wrigley family's ownership of the club that lasted until 1981 when the family sold the team to the current owners, the *Chicago Tribune*. Ironically, I am now an employee of the company that owns the Cubs, as the Tribune owns radio station WGN, the long-time flagship station of the Cubs.

I always referred to Philip Wrigley as "Mr. Wrigley." I called him Mr. Wrigley out of respect, not because I had to. He was a great man, a great owner.

Ernie Banks and Billy Williams were in a class by themselves, both on and off the field.

I know the New York media doesn't believe it, but Billy should have been elected to the Hall of Fame on the first ballot, like Ernie was. It is true that three of us never made it to the World Series; had we been able to get to the Fall Classic and get the inordinate amount of media attention associated with the game, things might have been different for all of us. Playing in postseason games puts a microscope on the team as well as the individuals. With so many newspapers and broadcasters looking for stories, it's inevitable that more is going to be written and said about those individuals. I wonder how much more attention across the country would have been paid to some of our players had we made it to the playoffs or the World Series.

Billy didn't have it easy. I'm not saying Ernie's life as a Cub was a cakewalk, but I know from experience the problems Billy faced as a black ballplayer. I came from an Italian neighborhood in Seattle. It was working middle class. It wasn't the bastion of liberal thinking, but we didn't know about segregation. When I was playing with San Antonio and met Billy during spring training, I had not encountered racial bias in my life until then. Maybe I was sheltered, probably I was lucky.

We had to go on a road trip early in the season, by bus, naturally. Billy was one of three black players on the team. But as we went on this road trip, the bus stopped and let Billy off.

At first I didn't understand. Billy didn't say anything. When we went down the road a bit and checked into our own hotel, I understood. Blacks didn't stay with whites, especially in the dusty minor league towns of the Lone Star State.

I never sat down and discussed this with Billy. I guess he understood what life was like in the late 1950s. We saw it on the major league level in the '60s as well, although not to this extreme.

One day at a home game in San Antonio, I arrived at the park for the usual routine of batting practice. Billy wasn't there. He had quit. He had gone home, despite his excellent stats and the Cub organization's belief that he would soon be a major leaguer.

To this day, I'm not one hundred percent certain of the details of Billy's short-lived retirement. But it didn't take a genius to figure out the scenario: the pressure of living apart from the rest of the team, the slurs he encountered from fans, both hometown and visitors. Billy was a proud man, something I sensed even on that level.

Buck O'Neal, a black coach and scout who signed Ernie Banks to his contract as the first black ever to play for the Cubs, was dispatched to talk to Billy. Whatever O'Neal said must have been persuasive. Billy came back without an explanation. I never sought one. I was probably too embarrassed to inquire. Whatever went through his mind, though, wound up being a Godsend not only for him, considering the mind-boggling numbers he put up during his major league career, but for the Cub organization. I can't fathom what our fortunes would have been during the 1960s, especially during 1969, without Billy Williams in the lineup.

Ernie was businesslike. He's known for the "let's play

two" and the constant sunshine personality, but on the field, he was an aggressive competitor and didn't joke around.

When Leo arrived in 1966, Ernie was 36 years old; not ready to be put out to pasture but hardly a rookie anymore. High on Durocher's agenda was to get Ernie to retire. He was jealous of the tremendous popularity and following Ernie had built with the Cub fans, not just in Chicago but across the country.

Durocher believed Banks was too laid back to play on one of his teams; he wasn't Gashouse Gang material. That's part of the myth about Ernie, possibly because the public only knows of his off-the-field personality.

I believed Durocher's attitude rejuvenated Ernie's career at the right time. It made Ernie more fiery on the field. After a disappointing 1966 campaign, Banks rebounded in 1967, the first year of our rebirth, to hit 23 homers and 95 RBI at age 37. Banks didn't care for Durocher but he didn't let that affect his play; in fact, it may have caused him to try to go that extra mile to prove that Leo was wrong about him.

Ernie was also a man with emotion, although I don't think the fans actually got to see the real Ernie Banks.

We were playing the San Francisco Giants one afternoon at Wrigley and were facing Jack Sanford, a guy who had hit Ernie Banks 12 different times in Banks's career. On Ernie's first trip to the plate he sent a homer into the left field stands.

The next time Banks came up, he was nailed right in the middle of the back. Banks walked slowly to first, and it was obvious he was in pain. He had to come out of the game as a precaution, even though it was next to impossible to get Ernie out of any inning of any game.

Ernie sat down on the bench and made a simple declaration: "I'll give $100 to the guy who gets to him," Banks announced.

At that moment, 24 other guys were ready to jump off

the bench to get Sanford. It was the only time in my entire career with Ernie that he was visibly upset.

What you saw publicly with Ernie was the way he was on the field and in the clubhouse. It wasn't a facade; he truly wanted to play two games every day, three if there had been enough sunshine at lightless Wrigley Field.

When the reporters could come in after a game at Wrigley and he had knocked a couple of homers out, he would go into a routine: "Say, do you know Mr. Williams and Mr. Santo?" Banks would ask the reporters, pointing to two lockers located right next to his. "You should be talking to those guys, fellas."

Always with a smile.

It seemed like Ernie would never give a straight answer to a reporter's direct question; after awhile, Billy and I would chuckle to ourselves when reporters would try over and over again to get some controversial quote from Ernie.

As I have traveled around baseball, first as a player and now as an announcer, I am saddened that Ernie is partly associated with being a great player who never got into postseason play. That he played on losing clubs. That's an unfair tag; it wasn't his fault any more than it was mine or Billy Williams.

I'm also of the opinion that today's players who get into postseason play—we didn't have divisional play until two-thirds through my career—don't appreciate what they are experiencing when they get into the playoffs or the World Series. I'm sure I'm speaking for Ernie by saying that; we would have loved to get in just once. But I'm sure we don't think of our careers or our achievements in any less of a light.

I had the privilege of playing alongside three Hall-of-Famers; it was an injustice it took so long for Ferguson Jenkins to get into the Hall of Fame. He was clearly the best pitcher in the history of the team. Season after season you knew you were going to get 200-plus innings plus 20 victories from him. He knew how to pitch at Wrigley Field. He didn't look for excuses when the wind was blowing out a gale to left field; he would simply just adjust his game.

What made Fergie so good was that he could locate a pitch anytime he wanted; he changed speeds better than anyone in the league. He didn't have the greatest fastball in baseball but could paint the outside corner.

Fergie also went out with a game plan each time. He knew what he wanted to do for nine innings before every start. We weren't blessed with great bullpens during my era and maybe Fergie was aware of that. He just expected to go nine innings every time out, and that is why he perennially led the league or was near the top of the league in complete games every year. I'm glad I didn't have to face Ferguson Jenkins in my career.

The four of us—Billy, Ernie, Fergie and I—made good money for our day; in the early 1970s, Billy and I were pulling down well over $100,000, near the top in the majors at the time. Today, it isn't even the minimum salary and is $900,000 BELOW the average salary of a major leaguer.

What would it have cost the Cubs or any team to pay the four of us if we were playing now? They probably couldn't afford to pay all four of us on the same team. There are guys making three or four million dollars now that don't even come close to the numbers the four of us put up for the Cubs. But the game is vastly different now; we never worried about the first and the 15th of each month (when players get their paychecks from the club). We honestly played it for the love of the game.

I don't know with today's economics and free agency whether the Chicago Cubs could have afforded to pay the salaries of the 1969 Cubs—we sure couldn't have been together on the same team for nearly a decade like we were. Besides having to pay the four of us, you would have had to come up with huge bucks to keep Glenn Beckert, Don Kessinger and Randy Hundley. So, in a sense, maybe it was good that we played in the era we did.

I will say this; if Mr. Wrigley thought it was the right thing to do, he would have paid whatever the market warranted to keep the team together. He was a generous man.

I might also add through all of my individual salary negotiations, I never had an agent. None of us did. Players during my era walked into the office, negotiated their contract face-to-face with management and shook hands. Maybe that is why there was a greater sense of loyalty on the part of players than there is today.

Usually I did most of my negotiations with John Holland, the general manager. It was clear he was working under the eye of Mr. Wrigley. One particular negotiation symbolized my working relationship with Mr. Wrigley. After the 1962 season, my wife and I wanted to buy a house in suburban Park Ridge. In order to buy the property, I needed a $12,000 down payment. Unbelievably inexpensive by today's standards, unbelievably expensive by 1962 standards.

I had made only $13,000 during the entire 1962 season so it was obvious I didn't have the money in the bank to afford this house. But we were like a lot of young couples during the early days of Camelot and the Kennedy administration; we saw a chance to get our dream house and we wanted to build for the future. We were intent on laying down roots in the Chicago area for what we hoped would be a long and fruitful career with the Cubs.

After a strong 1961 season, my first full one in the majors, I had a so-so season in 1962, although I knew the club still felt I was developing as one of the best fielding third basemen in the league. So when I went in to Holland to negotiate my contract for 1963, I had a strategy: I wouldn't ask for a raise but instead would seek a bonus of, you guessed it, $12,000, to cover the down payment on our home.

At the start of the negotiations, Holland said the $12,000 bonus was just too much money to give out to me. However, he did agree to talk to Mr. Wrigley about my special request.

Negotiations today in baseball can take weeks, even months. Not on this day. Holland stepped out of his office and went to Mr. Wrigley's office. He instructed me to step out into the hallway. After a 15 minute wait—it seemed like 15 hours— Holland returned.

"There's no way we can give you the $12,000 but we can give you $8,000," Holland explained.

I didn't have to think about my response. "Well, that's not going to work. I need the $12,000. John, I've been here two years and I'm going into my third full season and I'm going to be around this organization for a long time," I said. "Chicago is going to be my home, not Seattle. We want to put down some roots here and stay in the Chicago community."

Holland took even less time with his response. "Well, we just can't do it," Holland answered.

"Well, I can't sign it," I countered.

The negotiations were over.

Holland liked to have all of his players signed by January 15, something that doesn't happen now in baseball. The Cubs liked to have all of their players under contract by the time of the annual mid-winter Cubs luncheon where the players would meet the media as a sort of massive hot stove league session. But I wasn't signing without my $12,000.

I decided to attend the Cubs' mid-winter event even though I wasn't signed for the season. As I walked into the ballroom, I heard a voice call to me.

I turned around to see Mr. Wrigley. I had never met the man before, and although I had seen pictures of him, I was startled to hear the owner of the club and the leader of one of the largest companies in America call out to me.

"I understand we have a little problem?" Mr. Wrigley asked. "Come over here and let's have a little talk."

We went into a corner, away from the glare of the TV lights and microphones that were scattered all over the room. Reporters quickly broke away from their interviews with other players and noticed that I was having a private conversation with Mr. Wrigley.

"So, Ron, what's the problem?" he asked.

I'm sure I was nervous, talking to the boss and all, and didn't have the same bravado I had had in my conversations with Holland.

"Well, I have a home I want to buy in Park Ridge. I want to stay here, Mr. Wrigley, in Chicago," I explained. "I am not asking for a raise, just a bonus; call it an advance, Mr. Wrigley." I didn't know what to expect. He could have walked away or he could have written me a check on the spot.

"What do you need?" Mr. Wrigley asked, keeping the negotiations alive.

I only had to give a one-figure answer. "$12,000."

"Well, you meet me in my office in the Wrigley building at 9:00 A.M., tomorrow and John will be there and we will work it out," Mr. Wrigley announced. That was it? I had it? It was too good to be true. Wasn't it?

If I was nervous talking to Mr. Wrigley at the luncheon, I was petrified going in to his office to meet him face-to-face in the building that carries his family name. As I walked in, I couldn't help but notice this huge desk that he was working from; it probably would have covered the entire dining room in this home we wanted to buy.

We all shook hands, and Mr. Wrigley got straight down to business. "John and I talked it over and we know you're going to be around awhile, Ron, and I'd like to give you this check for $12,000,"

The smile on my face was as wide as the throw from third to first. I had gotten what I had asked for from the number one man.

But Mr. Wrigley wasn't through.

"And, Ron," he added, "we'd like to give you a raise—to $18,000."

I couldn't believe what I was hearing. They were giving me a 75 percent salary increase.

"Thank you," was all I could muster. I was flabbergasted. I couldn't wait to get home to tell my wife. We built that home. I have called Chicago my home ever since.

Owners often get criticized for a lot of things, particularly today. But I had one employer for 14 straight years, and the Wrigley family always took care of me and their players.

I'm still so sorry we didn't win a World Series for Mr. Wrigley; he deserved one.

eleven

The Other Side
of the Tracks

The thought that I would end my career with any team other than the Cubs was foreign to me. Even though I saw other mainstays like Fergie, Beckert and Kessinger depart, I still figured I would call it quits one day at Wrigley Field, say goodbye and disappear into the ivy.

But after the 1974 season, I knew something was up. Philip Wrigley, a man I respected and who I thought I had a good working relationship with, and John Holland were working on a deal. Holland was set to call me on the phone with the bad news.

He was blunt. They wanted to send me to the California Angels in a five-player deal. The Angels needed a veteran third baseman and were willing to part with four promising players.

"Ron, it's the toughest thing I've had to do since I've been here, but we're going to make this deal," said John Holland, who had been general manager since I joined the club. "I know you qualify for the reserve clause and have to agree with any deal. But we've got this deal with California and we need the two left-handers. It's up to you."

The deal made sense for the Cubs. They were rebuilding. It was obvious they were rebuilding with me. There wasn't a lot in the farm system (a situation that would haunt the Cubs into the 1990s) and getting four-for-one made sense. Holland made it clear the club was backing up the truck, and I wouldn't be the last to go.

But I didn't want to leave Chicago. My family was there. My business interests were there. My home was there. These were my roots after leaving Washington. The thought of spending six months away, especially on the West Coast, was a nightmare.

In the '60s and '70s, there was a thing called loyalty; I assumed that because I had been loyal to the Cubs they would be loyal to me. I had made it clear to the front office after the 1973 season that I was only going to play a couple of more years and I assumed it would be with the Cubs.

"I'm sorry, but no way can I go along with that deal," I said in a tone that was more informative than demanding. "John, I want to stay in Chicago to end my career." I continued, picking up steam. "First of all, I can't discuss this right now. My wife is ill—I had to take her to the hospital last night—and that's my number one concern. Call me in a week and we can maybe talk about it then." And I hung up.

Holland called me back a week later. But my feelings hadn't changed. "Listen John, things haven't changed. I'm just not going to California," I told him. I was tiring mentally by the end of the 1973 season. The thought of uprooting myself and my family was so unappealing. And like I said, I place a high price on loyalty. If I commit to something, either in business or in my personal life, people know that my word is my bond. I didn't want to be dealt, period. I figured I had given nearly two-thirds of my life to the Chicago Cubs' organization. I symbolized something to this franchise. And if they didn't want me anymore, I understood. But I wasn't going to be dished off to any team, let alone one 2,000 miles away, without having some say.

Then Holland posed a question that simply crushed me. "Well then," Holland asked, "where would you go?"

It was clear: It wasn't that they wanted this trade with the Angels; they wanted to get rid of number 10.

"Nowhere, John. I'll retire," was all I could say.

Holland said I couldn't do it, but I know he sensed my hurt.

The next day, Mr. Wrigley called. "Ron, we don't want you to go anywhere. We want you to stay here and help with the ballclub and help us with this new third baseman," Mr. Wrigley said, referring to a young Bill Madlock who was apparently ready to make it on the major league level.

But even though he was a man of power and a man I respected, my attitude hadn't changed. "Mr. Wrigley, I've spent 14 years here and I know that I'm not wanted anymore," I said. "I can't change my mind and I'm not even thinking of coming back just as a coach."

Harry Dalton, the GM of the Angels (he later went on to the Brewers) also tried to persuade me to accept the deal with his club. At the time, I was making $100,000 and he offered a sizeable raise. But by now, I considered myself financially sound; an off-season job with an oil company was giving me the security and the ability to tell Dalton the same thing I had told Holland and Mr. Wrigley.

My "veto" became a landmark in baseball. I was the first major leaguer in history to invoke what was then a new rule that allowed a 10-year man to veto any deal. I had been with the same club for 10 straight years and this gave me that right. The current so-called "5 and 10 rule" —five years with the same team, ten years in the majors—is an outgrowth of that and prohibits many teams from making deals with veteran players in the 1990s. When I did it, there were only 16 major leaguers with that right to veto the deal but no one had done it before. Now, vetoing of deals by veteran players is as common as a stolen base.

I thought my tactic would work. I felt confident I would be a member of the Chicago Cubs in 1974 and probably for the end of my career. I later found out Holland had made a similar plea with Billy Williams; Billy gave him the same answer.

Little did I realize the wheels were turning at Clark and Addison. Mr. Wrigley and Holland were still trying to think of ways to rebuild the club, to get it back to where it was in the late 1960s. They still wanted to make a deal for me.

Then the strangest thing happened. Chuck Tanner, then the manager of the White Sox who would go on to more success as skipper of the Pittsburgh Pirates, called me at home.

"Ron, I'm not supposed to be talking with you this way, but we would just love to have you over here," said Tanner, aware of the tampering rules that dictate in such situations.

I had liked Tanner from our chance meetings in the past and was naturally flattered that the Sox were interested. "First of all, Chuck, I'm not ready to come over to the American League and DH. You've got a third baseman already in Bill Melton. I'm only going to play a couple of more years, and it would probably not be worth your while for me to come over in a deal."

Tanner remained insistent. "I know all of that, Ron, but we'll play you at third and some at first. I also know you've played some left field in your career and we'll use you there. We're not talking about you being simply a DH," Tanner pitched. "We've got a good club here, and you can make it better."

I still couldn't see making such a move. "To be honest, Chuck, I don't think I could clear waivers and make it to you guys but thanks for the call."

But then I thought about it. What would the Cubs think about one of their longtime players going to the other side of town? I called Holland back. "Say, John, I've been thinking about what you have been telling me and I'm here to tell you I'll go along with a trade…" I paused, "…to the White Sox."

Holland didn't hesitate in his response. "No way, no way!" Holland said.

"Well, John, I've got to tell you, there is no way I'm going to be able to come back to the Cubs because you don't want me anymore."

I guess the Cubs and Holland were in a bind. Keep me and not get the pitching they needed or dispatch a local hero to the enemy. I hadn't told him Tanner had illegally called me, but I knew it wouldn't be long before talks would begin between the crosstown rivals.

I understand the rivalry in Chicago between Cubs and Sox fans. I have always sensed the Sox fans hate the Cubs fans more than vice versa. There seems to be a lot of resentment over the extra attention the Cubs have always received. Personally, I never had anything against the Sox when I was a Cub. Maybe because we were the big shots in town. To tell the truth, I honestly didn't pay much attention to what was going on with the Sox. I had some friends that played over there, but I wasn't paying much attention to their success or lack of it. But there was a great rivalry there between the fans and probably management, too. Both teams wanted to be number one in the city.

So when I heard some inkling that the Cubs started talking with the Sox, I guess I dismissed it at first. I didn't figure the Cubs would send a marquee attraction to help put paying customers in Comiskey Park and take them out of Wrigley Field.

I was wrong.

The deal was consummated on December 11, 1973. Ron Santo to the Chicago White Sox for pitchers Ken Frailing and Jim Kremmel, and catcher Steve Swisher. They also threw in a young right-hander by the name of Steve Stone, who, two decades later, would be working 20 feet away from me in a broadcast booth. Frailing and Kremmel were only with the Cubs briefly. Swisher alternated as the Cubs' number one and backup catcher for several years but never was the answer to the continuing search for a solid backstop like Randy Hundley.

The deal pushed Nixon, John Ehrlichman, Bob Haldeman, the White House Plumbers and Watergate off the front page, for that day at least. "Santo Dealt to White Sox" was the lead story. I guess it marked a return to page one for me for the first time since the Don Young affair.

Mr. Wrigley and Holland had given me the news the day before. Despite their change of tune that they didn't want to trade me, they knew now we had crossed the point of no return. I wanted out. I told them I understood their need to rebuild, especially the pitching staff. They were getting what they thought were three good young pitchers for me plus a catcher. I also told them I didn't want to be sent packing far away from Chicago. Well, they were complying. I didn't have to uproot my family or be away from my business.

But I was leaving the Cubs, and I'm sure to some it was like I was deserting the enemy. But I realized I basically had two options in the winter of '73. Retire or take the deal. Economically, the deal for me was too good to pass up. Two years, $260,000. Chicken feed for a marginal ballplayer today, big bucks in 1973. And the contract was guaranteed.

I was unfamiliar with the Sox personnel. Contrary to what you might think, living in the city of Chicago, I didn't follow what was going on with the Sox. Few of my teammates on the Cubs did. But I knew they had Melton, a power hitter with some decent defensive skills at third. Tanner made it clear from the first phone call I would be the third baseman with an occasional tour at first and left.

The combination of the money, Tanner's promises and the desire to still play the game made up my mind. Instead of an Arizona spring, I would, for the first time in my major league career, be headed toward Florida to train for an upcoming season. Heading to Sarasota at age 34, I knew I could still play. Maybe I could help this club and maybe it would all work out. In a sense I was both excited about playing in a new league and having a chance to get to the World Series with the White Sox.

When I arrived at Sarasota it finally hit me: I was on foreign soil. That first day was so strange; it was so weird to put on a different team's uniform after 14 seasons in Cubbie Blue. But little did I know the betrayal, frustration and hurt that would follow. I guess 1974 wasn't the best year for Richard Nixon or Ron Santo.

Right away, there was trouble. "Ron, we know what you can do so don't worry about spring training," said Tanner. "Oh, by the way, do me a favor. We want to give you a look-see at second," Tanner said in a matter-of-fact tone as he puts his arm around me. "Just stay away from third base." Right then and there, I knew I had made a mistake in accepting the deal. Tanner had broken his promise to play me at third. He could have been Paul Newman in the movie, *The Sting*, thumbing his nose at me. I had been conned.

I went crazy. "You're asking me to keep away from MY position? A position that I've been an All-Star at for 10 years?!"

"Well, Ron, Bill Melton is nervous about having you on the team. We're all major leaguers," Tanner said in his fatherly voice.

I told him I'd do it but I had gone from elation to deep

depression. I knew at that moment I would go out of the game quietly; I would play one last year and get out of baseball.

It wasn't that I thought I was above playing second; it was just that at that stage in my career, I didn't want to learn to play a whole new position. I had played second for one game during Leo's last year with the Cubs—I did it because I wanted to help the club and I was confident in a pinch I could play anywhere in the infield or outfield. Yet second base is a completely different position from third. The pivot on the double play, the way you station yourself for right-handed and left-handed hitters. I was a third baseman, a gold glover. And now Chuck Tanner was telling me to move over so they could keep Melton at third. And I also knew the Sox had a promising young second baseman named Jorge Orta, who would go on and have some productive seasons as an offensive threat for the club. What was I doing here?

I didn't speak out like I wanted to. But I did make it clear to Tanner I didn't come over to be a designated hitter. I didn't like DH-ing, didn't like the rule. I was a complete ballplayer and just taking four at-bats during a game didn't seem like playing baseball.

I also sought out Melton to try to ease his concerns; my years as captain of the Cubs convinced me this was the proper thing to do. And Bill seemed to accept the situation.

On Opening Day at Comiskey Park it was snowing, which I suppose was an omen. A large banner hung out in left field, "Welcome Ron Santo to the major leagues," as a not-so-subtle slap at my former team.

The 1974 Chicago White Sox were a pretty good club; we were picked to contend against the Oakland A's. Their promise of acquiring me to make a pennant drive seemed real enough. They had two terrific starters in Jim Kaat and knuckleballer Wilbur Wood. A young Bucky Dent was at short and a fellow by the name of Richie (he insisted on the first name Dick later on in his career) Allen at first.

Allen had been an MVP, and it was understandable why Tanner and the Sox believed he was the cornerstone of the team. Allen's reputation was one of a moody, introspective player. He's changed somewhat since his retirement; he wrote a book and does talk shows and is quite a bit more extroverted than he was when he was a player.

But I knew Allen had a reputation of dogging it when he felt like it; I had heard this from the teammates and managers he played with. I can tolerate a lot of things in a ballplayer, but not trying as hard as you can isn't one of them. Everyone is blessed with different abilities and gifts. In Allen's case, he was gifted; he had a tremendous swing and had the numbers to back it up. But on occasion, he wouldn't run out a grounder. Or he would flag at a ball hit to him and it would go into right for a single.

And here I was, wanting to play my heart out every day. The combination probably made things ripe for a confrontation.

Sitting on the bench one game at mid-year—I'm DH-ing which means I have plenty of time to observe—I noticed Allen was in his dogging mode again. He had forgotten how many outs there were and after a play at first, he tossed the ball to the umpire, allowing a run to score. There were only two, not three, outs. It was a close game.

I saw Allen go over to our pitcher that day, Jim Kaat, and apologize for messing up; he hit a homer the next inning as his way of saying he was sorry.

But his mental lapses would continue, and it irritated me. I'm sure I was mentally down because I was forced to DH, something I had dreaded from the first mention of the American League. I also disliked the American League atmosphere: In the National League, there was no fraternization among players on other teams; in the American League, it happened all the time. I didn't want to be pals with my opponents. And if that wasn't enough, the difference in the strike zone, which still exists today, was causing me fits.

I was an unhappy veteran.

The 1974 White Sox struggled out of the gate. The strain was showing on everyone.

And the Allen situation was starting to wear on the team. He would often show up at 7:45 P.M. for an 8:00 P.M. start. Well, I wasn't brought up to take your job for granted. But Tanner would let it go and continued to give Allen special treatment.

It came to a boiling point in a game in Minnesota. We were getting blown out. And Allen went up to Tanner and told him he couldn't take his at-bat. No reason, he just didn't want to hit. Tanner let it go, just like he'd been doing all year.

But I followed him down the steps into the clubhouse at the old Metropolitan Stadium.

"Tanner has been bending over backwards for you all year," I said, getting a season's worth of frustration out of my gut. He told me to get out of his face; he didn't have to answer to me. He reported to the manager, not to Ron Santo.

Again I told him what had been brewing in my mind for weeks: How does someone with his ability dare to not give it his best? Again, he yelled back that it's none of my business.

Well, it was my business. As a veteran on the Sox— remember, they had made the deal for me to give them a bat, glove and clubhouse leadership—I thought I was right to challenge him. He didn't see it that way.

We nearly came to blows. We had to be separated. I've never backed down from a fight in my life, even when the odds may not be with me. In Allen's case, the guy was a great physical specimen, which also contributed to my frustration with his lackadaisical play.

There were no actual fisticuffs. Tanner, for his part, could have and should have done more to rectify the situation. But Allen continued to get special treatment all year. I guess that's how he had been treated in Philadelphia, St. Louis and Los Angeles, and that was the way it was going to be here.

My lone year with the Sox was an unhappy one statistically. My numbers were awful: a .221 average with just five homers and 41 RBI in 117 games. All were significantly below my lifetime norms. I had another year on the contract but I couldn't face the prospect of a 1975 season being as bad as the one in 1974. The money was great but the aggravation wasn't going to be worth it.

The handwriting was on the wall. I could read it: it said, "Retire, Ron."

At the end of the year, I walked in to see John Allyn, who owned the team before Bill Veeck regained it for the last time in the mid 1970s, and I was frank.

"John, I appreciate all you've done for me this past year," I told him. "But I am going to retire."

"You have a two-year contract," Allyn countered. "All you have to do is stay one more year and you will get paid."

"You've got it wrong, John. I'm retiring."

"You're going to give me $130,000 back for not playing?" he asked in an incredulous tone. "No player has ever walked away from that kind of money."

My answer was firm and airtight. The thought of going to another club was never even a consideration.

Ironically, the 1975 Sox would drop to fifth place, 22 games out. Allen was dealt off that club back to the Phillies and was out of baseball by 1977. Tanner would also leave the Sox after 1975, heading off the embarrassment that waited for him in 1976 when the Sox lost 97 games and wound up in the basement of the American League West.

I had made the right decision at the right time. I have never regretted it.

twelve

Pizza Man

I never had the benefit of a college education, but that was not uncommon in major league baseball. Unlike football or basketball, you have to impress the scouts in your teens. Baseball didn't have the mechanism by which you could go ahead and finish your college education and not fall behind others trying to make it on a roster.

So when I signed out of high school with the Cubs, I was aware of the post-baseball risks. I saw, and have seen, athletes filled with optimism and vigor that they would be able to play baseball forever. Father Time wouldn't ever catch up to them. Their bodies would take care of them, making a living without having to worry about the future. Right.

I was fortunate. Early in my major league career I wanted to make plans for the time when I wouldn't play baseball any more. I'm sure I had some of the same bravado as any one who has played the game: that I would play for a long time. But I wanted to be ready.

After my second year with the Cubs, I was approached about opening a pizza parlor. This was before the days of the franchising success of a Domino's or Pizza Hut. I had the right Italian name and the right recipe (from my mother) so I invested a small amount of money, lent my name and I was off.

Santo's Pizza opened up in suburban Park Ridge, Illinois, a combination pizzeria and delivery system. I was determined even then to be involved with the venture, unlike so many of the current restaurants that have an athlete's name but where the athlete never appears at the establishment. I do the same thing at my restaurant, Ron Santo's, that operates in suburban Schaumburg today.

I actually learned how to prepare the pizza; I wasn't a gourmet chef but I wanted to learn the business from the crust on up. The product was good; Cub fans were willing to give it a try, and it was a success. We did very well, especially at first. During home games, I would make a trek nearly every day to see how the business was doing.

One Saturday night, I got a call from one of my weekend managers. It seemed our delivery man was out sick, and we were getting besieged with orders. I told my guy not to worry; I'd come down in my car, take the pizzas out and make the deliveries myself. I lived five minutes from the place, so it didn't sound too difficult.

Here I was, a major league third baseman, making pizza deliveries in my Cadillac but I knew it was essential to keep the customers happy and loyal. Being a famous athlete doesn't replace the taste of cold pizza. Armed with a roadmap, I was halfway through my deliveries—geography was never my strong subject—when I knocked on the door of one customer who had about a half dozen or so party revelers.

"Sir," I told him, "your pizza is here."

He wasn't pleased. "The pizza is an hour late," he snarled. "I wanted it on time."

The aroma of the pizza probably soothed his nerves and calmed his stomach. He cooled down. Then, after he paid me, he asked me a favor.

"Could you get the owner, this Ron Santo guy, to autograph a baseball for my son? He's not well and would appreciate it. Besides, he owes us for having this pizza late," the guy pointed out.

Obviously, this guy wasn't a die-hard Cub fan. I suppose I was humbled a bit myself.

"I'm Ron Santo and I'd be happy to sign the kid's baseball," I boasted.

"You are NOT Ron Santo! Ron Santo wouldn't be delivering pizzas on a Saturday night!" he insisted. Eventually, I finally convinced him who I was. I signed the ball, got the money for the pizza and left. I don't remember if I got a tip.

The business seemed to be flourishing. I was approached to consider franchising Ron Santo's pizza. We opened up six other establishments around the area. The "pizza man" had been born.

The next year, I had an idea: why not sell my pizza at Wrigley Field? I got the idea at Shea Stadium, certainly not one of my favorite places, when vendors brought in some big, warm slices of pizzas into the clubhouse instead of the usual cold cuts. It dawned on me on the flight home that it would be a novel idea to have pizza at Wrigley Field. Remember, this was the mid 1960s before the sophisticated bill-o-fare of today's stadiums. Hot dogs, beer, peanuts and cracker jack were standard items; nachos, gourmet wieners and fancy sandwiches were years away.

I was told I would have to approach Philip K. Wrigley, owner of the team. I had talked to him on a couple of previous occasions but it was strictly baseball related. We would talk contract or about the general progress of the Cubs, not pizza. And even though I had faced Sandy Koufax's fastball and line shots from the bat of Willie Mays at third base, I was nervous meeting Mr. Wrigley about the pizza proposition.

I was surprised to hear him answer his own phone.

"Mr. Wrigley, can I come up and see you on a business idea that I have come up with?" I asked as the receiver was trembling in my hand.

"Sure, Ron, come on up," he said. I was breathing easier.

We arranged a meeting, and I met with him at his office at Wrigley Field. He was very courteous and made me feel at home from the moment I walked in to see him. He said he was aware of the success my pizza establishments had in the area. I told him of my plans to have my pizza sold at Wrigley Field. I explained that the Cubs wouldn't have to do much work. We would prepare the pizzas, par-baking them and deliver them daily to the ballpark. The ovens would complete the process at the park so the pizzas would taste fresh, not like the cardboard tastes of other pre-prepared pizzas.

He bought the idea. It didn't hurt that we had some of my teammates agree to have their faces on the cover of the pizza boxes. A sort of baseball card but instead of the gum, you got pepperoni. We gave each teammate $200 for the rights to use their faces on the covers.

I sold the pizzas to the concessionaires; cheese pizza went for 25 cents, sausage for 40 cents. Great price, great pizza. It got to be so big that I couldn't make enough pizzas to supply the demands. I went to a manufacturer to assist in making the pizza, it was that big of a business. All of the money we were making went back into the business because I had my baseball salary to live on.

We eventually went into Chicago area supermarkets to get the frozen product in under the name "Pro's Pizza." I eventually sold the pizza business after eight years.

But at least I knew when I retired after the ill-fated season with the White Sox that I would have to do something else. Then a local oil company approached me about being in their firm. I knew nothing about residual oil sales and marketing, but officials of the firm said they would teach me what I needed to know. And they did. I learned the business, eventually reaching vice president of sales. I loved the work, the personal contacts, everything about it. The firm would purchase oil in the Gulf Coast area, bring it up by barge and would sell it to large industrial firms, particularly major steel companies.

I didn't mind being behind a desk part of the time. I loved traveling to the various steel mills, meeting people, wining and dining them and getting to see the country. Sure, there were people who knew who Ron Santo was but when it comes to the big business of selling oil, they were concerned with product, not that I had .277 lifetime average and 342 career home runs.

During my first year of retirement, I didn't attend many Cubs' games. I followed their progress but I didn't care much for being in big crowds so I generally stayed away from Wrigley Field. Upon reflection, I guess when I retired I just wanted to stay away from the game as much as I could.

Eventually, I left the oil company. I considered going to the Chicago Board of Trade to start another new career in 1976, but then I sat down with two other sales people and a supply man who had also left the same oil company. We thought we could make it on our own with our own business.

We called the company Nova Oil. We borrowed $1.5 million to get the thing started, a lot of money back in 1976 (and a lot of money now). We were confident we could make a go of it and apparently the bank agreed. The risks were great; had it failed, I would have been financially ruined.

It was beginning to be a difficult time for me personally. I was putting in very long hours to get this venture off the ground and it took me away from my home and family a lot, much the same as baseball had done.

It was very difficult on my marriage. Being a baseball wife isn't easy; the demands on a player's time and the "opportunities" that were out there could put a strain on even the best marriages. Earlier in my marriage, we had a rocky period in the mid-1960s when at one point, I actually moved out of our home. We patched things up and had our third child, a lovely daughter, Linda, in 1969. It was the high point of the year, right ahead of Neil Armstrong landing on the moon.

But all of a sudden, Judy and I started to grow apart. We had married right out of high school, something I would counsel against for today's teens. We just didn't realize that we didn't have a lot in common. It was no one's fault. These things just happen.

But I was living with the memory of a traumatic exit by my father at age seven; even at that age, I vowed I would never walk out on my children and would never get divorced. But I had to come to terms with the fact that our marriage was over. I changed my thinking about divorce, although I never strayed from my commitment to be a full-time father to my three children. As with most divorces, it didn't happen overnight; our commitment to our children caused us to wait and finally we got the decree in 1982.

I met Vicki Tenace at a riding stable in Lake County, Illinois. Ever since I was a kid I loved horses—secretly I always wanted to be Gene Autry, a rootin', tootin' cowboy (without the singing, please). Riding was a great way for me to have a release—early in my career when I lived near Wrigley Field I would head toward the suburbs and rent a horse each day to relax.

Vicki and I were riding companions at first; she didn't even recognize who I was when we first got to know one another. The friendship eventually transformed into romance, and we were married in September 1982. To this day, she is still my best friend as well.

Businesswise, we eventually paid back the loan for the new business and my three other partners bought me out in 1981, the year before Vicki and I got married.

I turned then to another business venture, Interpoint Corporation, which was involved in truck stops, with three other different partners. I also got involved with some Kentucky Fried Chicken franchises in the Chicagoland area.

My contact with the Cubs was relegated to watching them on television or reading about them in the newspaper. I was about as far away from baseball during the early 1980s as I had been during my entire life.

In 1987, WGN radio reached back and took a chapter from the Charlie Grimm-Lou Boudreau booth-to-manager switch. Jim Frey, who had been fired early in the 1986 season by Dallas Green, had been hired to do color commentary with DeWayne Staats and Harry Caray. After one year on the job, Frey, in a surprise move, was brought back to replace Dallas Green as vice president and general manager.

That left an opening in the broadcast booth. The station approached me about coming down for an audition. Actually, the thought of broadcasting Cubs' games wasn't at the top of my priority list at the time. I had been involved in a successful, full-time business. I had Vicki, my three children were now adults, and I had made a full life for myself.

WGN first became interested in me around 1987, but I told them my business commitments would make it difficult to broadcast a 162-game season. So they hired Jim Frey.

I threw out the pitch before one of the '89 playoff games and the electricity generated by the evening sparked an interest. I believed the Cubs were on the verge of having a great team and I wanted to be in some small way a part of it because of our near-miss in 1969.

WGN was completely revamping its booth; Staats had gone on to a job with the New York Yankees. They invited me down to Florida to do a mock broadcast; I had never done one minute of announcing before then. I went off to the now-defunct Senior Professional Baseball League to audition.

They paired me with Bob Brenly, the former San Francisco Giant catcher who had done some broadcasting during his playing career. Thom Brennaman, whose dad I had known as the voice of the Cincinnati Reds, was the play-by-play guy. Don Albert was our engineer and a big help to me.

I had doubts whether I would be able to succeed on the level I had as a player or a businessman. I had been out of the game for nearly 15 years. My solution was to do what I did when I first learned I had diabetes: read and study. I cannot emphasize enough to young people the importance of reading. I read as much as I could about the current Cubs and the National League in general.

I announced the first four-and-one-half innings, Brenly called the next four-and-one-half.

I knew Brenly and I were vying for the same job; normally in such cases, there would be an unspoken tension. Instead, we got along great. We ate dinner together and exchanged views. I know, no fraternization, but in this case, it was fine.

Brennaman also did everything he could to make it easy for me. I knew that Brenly and Brennaman had been friends, and they could have made me feel like an outsider but they did just the opposite. I had talked to Johnny Bench before the audition about the situation, and he told me that Thom, like Marty, was a professional and a nice human being. He was right on both counts. Somehow, we had instant chemistry among the three of us. It was like walking into a room and meeting two old friends.

I did the broadcasts and was uncertain of whom they would choose. "Listen, Bobby, whoever gets the job, I want you to know something, especially if I don't get it," I said to Brenly. "We're playing golf the next time we see one another."

About a month later, I got the call from WGN general manager Dan Fabian and program director Lorna Gladstone. I had gotten the job. But so had Brenly. And Brennaman was the man who would do play-by-play. We had a three-man broadcast booth.

From the minute of the first day of spring training until the end of the season, I continued to do my homework. I knew I wasn't a professional announcer so I wanted to be prepared. I'd come early to the ballpark, introduce myself to the players from BOTH teams and try to get as many inside tips as I could. When it would be my turn to talk in the booth, I wanted to sound authoritative.

I'm sure my first year was a bit rocky, beginning with my ill-fated opening words when the coffee spilled. It was a transition that seemingly hundreds of other ex-players have made but it was a learning process for me. To be honest, I didn't think I was very good. I felt out of place at times in the booth. Thom and Bob helped me whenever they could; they were both professionals and did everything in their power to give me the opportunity to succeed.

What I found the most difficult wasn't knowing what to say but when to say it; the toughest adjustment into announcing is knowing when NOT to talk, rather than when to talk.

The second year, in 1991, I thought I had improved and felt more comfortable. We were clicking as a team; nothing was forced.

After the 1991 season, Brenly headed back to San Francisco to serve as a coach under Roger Craig. I think Brenly wants to become a major league manager someday, and he's going to be a very good one whenever he gets the opportunity.

In 1992, it would be just Tommy and me. I knew I would have to do more talking and be on top of everything that went on inside the clubhouse and on the field. I continued to pitch occasional batting practice with the team and learned as much as I could about the Cubs' opponents.

The chemistry was still there between Brennaman and me; it also continued between Harry Caray and me for the three middle innings he does. For his part, Harry jokes around with me and talks more about my playing days. After all, he was there with the St. Louis Cardinals during my first 10 years with the Cubs and of course, during 1969. Thom was still in grammar school, but it is amazing the knowledge he has about baseball back then. Of course, it didn't hurt to have a father in the booth as his tutor.

I know it has become fashionable for announcers, particularly talk show hosts, to rip players for mistakes that they make. I have a strict philosophy on this; I'm not going to tear in to some guy on the radio or TV for a physical mistake. I played the game and I understand those things can happen. Announcers who go after guys on this side of things are way off. But if a guy is dogging it mentally and isn't hustling or trying; then he's fair game.

Make no mistake, I root for the Cubs. I have since my early days in Seattle and I'm a big fan now. When the club is going well, I'm slapping my hands together and I'm happy as a clam. When the Cubs are in a slump, I'm down about it.

Yet, I'm not afraid to speak my mind if any player, including a Cub, doesn't run out a ground ball or is lackadaisical in the field. I didn't play the game that way and I don't think it should be played that way today.

thirteen

Who's the Best?

The Cubs didn't win the pennant the year after I was dealt to the White Sox; they didn't win it the year after I retired, either. But you already knew that, didn't you? In fact, entering the 1993 season, the Cubs still hadn't won the National League pennant since 1945, the year World War II ended and Harry Truman was in the White House.

They haven't won the World Series since 1906. Teddy Roosevelt was in the White House that year.

To a certain extent, part of the hangover from 1969 was erased when the Chicago Cubs won the National League Eastern Division in 1984. I was thrilled for them and also particularly thrilled they held off the New York Mets to win that flag.

At the time, I was inundated with calls for interviews about 1969 and our near-miss, and about my views on the 1984 club. At first, the calls were just from Chicago; then media from all over the country started to call and ask the same questions.

During the National League playoffs, I was hired to do a Miller Lite commercial with Norm Cash of the Tigers, Randy Jones of the Padres and Paul Splitorff of the Kansas City Royals—we represented the four teams in the post season playoffs that year. It was going to be a special spot for the World Series: whichever two teams went to the World Series, Miller would use our portion of the commercial.

They flew us out to New York for an audition and then they flew us all to Philly to some local bar. We all did the same commercial; mine was supposed to be set in Chicago. I can't remember if I was "tastes great" or "less filling." We filmed the first commercial after the Cubs swept past the San Diego Padres at Wrigley Field 13-0 in the first game, and it appeared that the Cubs were headed to the Series.

When word came back the next day that the Cubs had won again, the extras wearing Cubs' uniforms in my commercial were feeling great; we had a two-games-to-nothing lead, and it appeared our commercial would be the one airing on the World Series.

And then the Padres won the third game.

Still, I was confident it was going to end on Saturday night with Rick Sutcliffe on the mound. My wife Vicki and I were in Phoenix having dinner at Don & Charlie's; I was so optimistic I didn't even feel the need to spend the night in front of a TV. I didn't know when I made the dinner reservation that Manager Jim Frey wasn't going to start Sutcliffe.

Periodically, we would ask our waiter to give us updates and finally we walked over to the bar…just in time to see Steve Garvey hit that homer in the ninth off Lee Smith to square the series.

Still, I was confident the Cubs would win that fifth and deciding game, and my commercial would make it to the airwaves.

Well, if you're reading this book, you know the rest. The Cubs lost. I am convinced to this day that if Sutcliffe had pitched in game four, the series would have ended. Instead, the momentum switched to the Padres, and they won. My commercial ended up on the cutting room floor, along with my optimism.

I know some people thought our Class of '69 was somehow jealous of the success the 1984 National League Eastern Division winners received. Nothing could be farther from the truth. It might have been difficult to have all the comparisons conjured up again as that team drove for the division title. Who was better, 1984 or 1969? I was asked that all of the time.

My mind hasn't changed.

I don't like comparisons but I thought we had the better club. In fact, I always considered the 1984 Cubs to be a lot like the 1969 Mets because so many veteran Cubs' players had career seasons that year, performances they never duplicated. I've never felt the 1969 Mets had better personnel than we did. I don't think the 1984 Cubs did either.

Look at the lineups:

We had Ernie Banks at first base, a perennial all-star and Hall-of-Famer. They had Leon Durham, a potentially dangerous hitter but not in Ernie's league.

We had Beckert at second and even though he was my roommate, I'd give the nod to Ryne Sandberg who had an MVP season that year and is truly the greatest second baseman I've ever seen.

Don Kessinger at short would rate over Larry Bowa. Kessinger did so many things well and covered a lot more ground than Bowa did.

Third base? Sure, I'm prejudiced but I'll take Ron

Santo over Ron Cey. Look at my numbers in '69: 29 homers, 123 RBI, a Gold Glove. Cey had a good year, too, in '84, with 25 homers, 97 RBI. But you can do the math.

In the outfield, we had Billy Williams in left. Again, a Hall-of-Famer who played every inning of every game, hitting for power and batting. 293. Gary Matthews at right was a solid RBI man, great with two outs. But Matthews is no Billy Williams.

Jim Hickman at right had good numbers and had come into his own. Hick was a better fielder with a rifle arm that gives him the nod over Keith Moreland. In center, Bobby Dernier of the '84 club was the table setter and deserves the nod over Don Young. Dernier had better numbers and was a much scarier threat on the basepaths.

The pitching? Well, Fergie won 21, Bill Hands 20, Kenny Holtzman 17 and Dick Selma 10. The 1984 Cubs had Rick Sutcliffe go 16-1 and was as dominant as Fergie was during our 1969 run. But Steve Trout, Scott Sanderson and Dennis Eckersley, before he went on to become the premier relief pitcher in the league with the A's, couldn't match Hands and Holtzman.

Actually, I thought the 1989 Cubs were better than the '84 team. Mark Grace and Shawon Dunston strengthened the club at first and short, and Andre Dawson was far superior to Keith Moreland. Greg Maddux certainly fell within the Fergie-Sutcliffe range but that 1989 club might not have had as much pitching as ours. I liked the 1989 club a lot; I have always admired Don Zimmer and his managerial skills. He was aggressive and always willing to take a chance as a player; he was the same way as a manager. It paid off for him during the 1989 season when he often went against the book. Still, the 1989 team, which lost to the San Francisco Giants in five games of the National League championship series, was not as strong as our 1969 club.

For some reason, the 1969 Cubs remain a black hole

for many Cub fans and some front office types. I bristle at anyone who brands us "losers." It angers me to hear that, particularly in Chicago.

I remember when Dallas Green came over from Philadelphia to become GM of the club when the Tribune bought the team from the Wrigleys. Green made it clear to anyone and everyone he didn't want any part of the 1969 team's legacy; we were "losers" in his mind, and he didn't want his club associated with a bunch of "losers." I also recall a local sportscaster on our own Cubs' station spouting off the same way on Green's weekly talk show. I was furious but I let it pass; that's just a part of the enduring legacy. But I did think Green's comments were a cheap shot because they perpetuated the wrongful myth that the 1969 club (and the years immediately preceding and following) were dark days for the organization. Nothing could be further from the truth, and a look at the stat sheet proves my case. Since we last finished as a .500 club in 1972, the team has finished over .500 just twice in two decades: the 1984 and 1989 division winning teams. Yet between 1967 and 1972, we finished above .500 EVERY year. We must have been doing something right for a bunch of guys Green and others considered as "losers."

And while Green deserves credit for building the club that would eventually win in 1984—he was the one that made the great deal to bring Ryne Sandberg from the Phillies to the Chicago Cubs—he wasn't able to wipe away the memories Cubs' fans had of that great summer in 1969.

Randy Hundley, who had been a fine manager in the Cubs minor league organization before Green's tenure, got hurt a lot more than I ever did from Green's philosophy. One of the first things Green did when he took over was to fire Hundley, who I always thought would make an excellent major league manager. But the bottom line was that anything related to '69 was jinxed and had to go.

Walk through the bleachers this summer and ask fans

which team was the greatest. I bet they say our '69 club. We didn't win it all, yeah, I know all about that. But my guess is that in the year 2010, people will still be talking about our 1969 club and the players on it; other teams and other players may fade from memory, but ours won't.

Jim Frey, Green's field manager in '84 and subsequently the man who took over for Green as general manager, echoed Green's feelings about our club. Supposedly Frey was asked whether they would ever hold a reunion or old-timers' game for the 1969 club and he shrugged it off, saying he didn't see why anyone would want to honor a team that lost. Well, if he doesn't see why, he should be there when we all get together and re-live the memories on our own, both privately and at Hundley's fantasy camps, where people pay thousands of dollars to suit up and play against Ernie, Billy, me and a bunch of other relics from '69. And by the way, the popularity of those camps offers additional proof of the love affair that continues between us and our fans.

In 1984, a group in Phoenix, Arizona, wanted to stage a "dream" game between members of the 1969 New York Mets and the Chicago Cubs for a local charity. In essence, they wanted us to relive 1969.

I told the organizers I was having eye trouble and couldn't play. It was true, but my feelings ran deeper than that. There was just too much hurt.

Some of my old teammates wanted to get me to change my mind, but I wouldn't budge.

I have always felt the Mets were arrogant, even cocky, about their winning in 1969, particularly down the stretch; you couldn't help but feel they were rubbing our faces in it. I seemed to be their favorite target, and they weren't ashamed to let me know their contempt. It was not classy.

I felt that playing in this "rematch" game would only conjure up bad memories for me. Not of the 1969 season, but of the Mets. They wanted to stick it down our throats again, and I wanted no part of it.

They went ahead and staged the game without me, and I don't regret missing it. I watched a couple of innings of the exhibition on television, then turned it off. I had made the right decision.

Actually, I don't know what would have happened if we had won back in 1969 and beaten out the Mets; the legacy might not have been as great. We related to the fans like no other Cub team has done since; we didn't have a fence around our cars at Wrigley Field like they do now. We knew the Bleacher Bums by their first names; we related to the fans; we needed the fans. And can you name another team, maybe other than the Dodgers, who had as many guys stick together as a unit as we did for nearly a decade? Normally in baseball, the phone rings and the player is out the door. Not our team. We were close on and off the field.

It's hard for teams in the '90s to put together the kind of lineup we had back in the '60s; since 1968, six new teams have been added to the National League (the Mets, Expos, Padres and Astros in 1969, and the Rockies and Marlins in 1993). How these new teams will do is anyone's guess, but it will further dilute the game, that's for sure. The talent just isn't there to go around for 28 major league baseball teams. When I started, there were only 18 clubs. You've nearly doubled the number of clubs but the number of quality major league players hasn't doubled.

Money has affected the thinking of players on all clubs. They just don't approach the game the way they did when I started my major league career more than three decades ago. Long-term deals which seem to be the rule rather than exception are hurting baseball. How many players do you see tail off after they sign a three- or four-year deal with guaranteed money? They don't bust their butt the way they miraculously do in their option year. Multi-year contracts just didn't exist when I played and I think it reflected in the quality of the game. Combine that with expansion and you have a diluted product.

People love to say that free agency is hurting the game, but I say that arbitration is the villain. Let's not point the finger at that elite group of superstar players earning five, six, seven million a year—those players put fans in the seats and give the game its glow. No, let's take a look at the large number of players with average ability earning two million dollars a year because of arbitration. That's what is hurting the owners and the game.

And even though the money for players is more than we ever could have dreamed of back in the '60s and early '70s, I'm proud to have been a part of baseball in my era. Baseball was at its peak then, and I had the opportunity to play with and against some of the greatest players ever to play the game. I'll stack up our teams and our accomplishments against any in any period since then.

Did I want to win and beat the Mets and get into the playoffs? You bet. I wasn't thinking of it in monetary terms or whether it would bring me a four- or five-year contract with big dollars. I wanted to win for winning's sake.

fourteen

Side Effects

When the doctors first told me that I had juvenile diabetes, I was warned about the possible side effects. I lived with that concern throughout my playing days, throughout my life. But despite all of the precautions that you can take, the disease will sometimes have its way.

During my career, I never had a problem with my eyes. But after my retirement, Dr. Jacob Suker, who had remained my doctor and close friend, warned me to constantly regulate my insulin, watch my weight and keep in shape. So many athletes I knew had let their bodies go; I was determined not to be a candidate for the "before" and "after" ad with a spare tire around my stomach. To this day, I maintain a constant workout regimen, due to my desire to stay fit and avoid any complications from diabetes.

In 1982, a full eight years after my retirement, I was out doing some horseback riding—one of my favorite pastimes—at the Blue Ribbon stables where I met an opthamologist, Dr. Ozzie Lopez. We got to talking about a lot of things, including my disease, and he asked whether I was getting regular eye checkups. I said yes but acted upon his suggestion to have another eye exam.

Maybe Dr. Lopez knew something, because upon further review, it appeared that there were changes in my eyes. I had developed retinopathy, a disorder caused by the diabetes which has the potential to damage the retina, the part of the eye that is connected to the brain by the optic nerve.

Dr. Lopez referred me to another doctor who suggested that laser surgery on my right eye would be needed. Apparently, there had been some bleeding in the eye; the laser would go in between where the vessels had ruptured, and give more oxygen to the new vessel to eventually improve the situation.

Naturally, I was concerned. Any time there is a problem with your eyes, you have to wonder: Could I go blind? Enough experts had told me the laser procedure was safe, so I was less concerned about that. But I was very much worried about the change in my eyes and the possibility of losing my sight permanently.

Before 1970, the diagnosis for retinopathy caused by diabetes was that you could be legally blind after three years, totally blind after five years. But with the advent of laser surgery, there was the potential to stem the damage and save the eyes.

To me, there was no alternative; I had to have the laser surgery, something I did at Michael Reese Hospital in Chicago in 1982.

Usually, if one eye is having problems, the other one would follow. Sure enough, I started to experience problems with the left eye. I needed laser surgery on the left eye. Actually, the laser treatment was painless. The scary part is when you put your head in the machine. I continued the treatment over a period of months and things seemed to be stabilizing, although the laser treatment would not cure proliferative retinopathy, it would just control it. I wound up with about 4,500 laser burns in my right eye, 4,000 in the left eye.

Currently, I have my eyes checked every six to nine months. I had my last laser treatment in 1989 and fortunately, the problems are in remission. I still wear glasses but that is not connected to the retinopathy or the diabetes.

I had gone from having better than 20-20 vision during my career, to as bad as 20-40 during the laser treatment. Now it's back to 20-30.

The technology that is being developed is miraculous; one doctor told me about a procedure whereby they actually freeze one eyeball and do additional laser work, a procedure I didn't need to have, fortunately. But such advances could only have been accomplished by the tremendous amount of research being funded by money raised by the federal government and the Juvenile Diabetes Foundation.

Shortly after I retired from major league baseball, I received a call from Sue Ellen Johnson in Chicago, a mother whose four-year-old daughter had juvenile diabetes. She was working together with area mothers and fathers whose children had contracted the same disease that I had been afflicted with. Her work along with others helped found the Juvenile Diabetes Foundation (JDF).

JDF was working on a fund-raising walkathon in the Chicago area to help raise badly-needed funds to help fight the disease. They wanted to call it the "Ron Santo Walkathon," and volunteers would solicit contributions from various neighborhoods for diabetes research. I welcomed the opportunity to lend my name to both the walkathon and JDF. When I was first diagnosed with the disease back in the late

1950s in Seattle, there was no money going toward research for a cure, and it seemed unlikely that there would ever be one in my lifetime. Now, the effort was being undertaken for research to try to find a cure.

I was already aware the American Diabetes Association was doing great work in this area, teaching diabetics how to live and cope with the disease; Sue Ellen Johnson said parents had been getting together since 1974 to try to convince the federal government to allocate funds to the National Institute for Health for the purpose of researching juvenile diabetes and finding a cure.

Since its beginning, different JDF chapters have raised more than $60 million. Our first walkathon that started in Wheeling, Illinois, raised about $40,000, a lot of money for a first go-round. We actually went over the $120,000 mark in 1992.

Even before the public disclosure that I was a diabetic, I made private visits to various local hospitals to visit people with diabetes. To this day, I still get phone calls from around the country from parents whose children have been diagnosed with diabetes. Their request is usually the same: would I write a letter to their child and tell them about my experiences of overcoming the disease and becoming a major league baseball player.

The letters are important, but whenever possible, I try to make a personal call to the children, and I try to relate my experiences. I try to alleviate the fears associated with diabetes. The most common fear in the minds of youngsters is the fear of having to take a shot. Unless you have been young and ill with such a disease, you can't appreciate the apprehension that can exist in the mind of a youngster in this condition. We all pray that our children stay healthy forever; we want to think of them as indestructible and immune from any malady. When diabetes strikes, it is important to learn about the disease and the side effects. This is what I tell the children; this is what I tell the parents.

The stories of courage of the young people I've met could fill a book in itself. More than 12 million Americans have been diagnosed with diabetes, and each person has stories of how he or she dealt with the disease. But the children who have juvenile diabetes have a special place in my heart.

When I was playing with the Cubs, I paid a visit to a Holiday Home camp in Wisconsin, where campers from the age of 6 to 16 with diabetes spend three weeks together. Nurses would be there but parents would not. It was like any camp where kids could swim, play ball, have fun. The main difference here was that the children were learning they were not alone, that other people their age faced the same problems and took their daily shots just like they did every day.

It was a motivating experience for me. I spent the entire day there, talking to the campers, playing softball, and exchanging stories. At the end of the day, I spoke to the group in an auditorium.

As I was getting ready to leave at the end of the day, a little boy came up to me and tugged at my pants leg. At first, I didn't see him. Then he looked up at me and said something that has stayed with me to this day:

"Gee, Mr. Santo, I'm sure glad you are a diabetic."

It was hard not to be touched by that gesture.

Every day for the last 35 years, I have gone through the regimen of giving myself a shot of insulin. As an adult, it has become as common for me as brushing my teeth. I was lucky; giving myself a shot was never a serious problem. Imagine, however, if you are a four- or five-year-old and you have to get a shot every day. What child isn't afraid of getting a yearly tetanus or flu shot? Imagine what it must be like every day. It is especially tough on the parents. They don't want to see their children go through such an ordeal. It's a traumatic experience.

In my discussions with parents, I try to emphasize how

important it is for the child to eventually give himself his own shot. By the time diabetics are six or seven, they should start doing it themselves. There is a tendency to drift toward denial as a teenager, and some skip the daily shots. Learning to do it themselves helps them understand what is at stake.

By the way, I'm not the only person with diabetes to have an active, physical life. Jackie Robinson, the Hall-of-Famer who broke the color barrier back in the 1950s with the Brooklyn Dodgers, had diabetes and had to fight off serious eye problems before his death. Former Chicago Bear Mike Pyle was diagnosed at age 25; we discussed the problems of traveling, regulating your insulin and the general adjustments a professional athlete would have to make because of the disease. Hall-of-Famer Jim "Catfish" Hunter, who helped lead the Oakland Athletics to those three straight world series titles in the early 1970s, found out at age 33 that he had diabetes. It shows that it can happen to people at an advanced age. Bill Gullickson, who came up with Montreal and now pitches for Detroit, has pitched throughout his professional career with diabetes. Bobby Clarke, the great Philadelphia Flyer, has diabetes and has had a tremendous career in the National Hockey League.

Like with any disease, there are often misunderstandings and sometimes unwarranted prejudice toward those with the disease. I have talked to people outside of sports who have had difficulty getting or securing work because they are diabetic. Personally, I was fortunate; I never have had any personal experiences with prejudice for this disease.

The number one question I usually get from parents and children alike is how I was able to play for so long in professional baseball and still had to take the shots. I never made a big deal of it when I was playing in the majors. I would usually get up in the morning, take the shot in the leg and drink some orange juice. I would then go back to bed as if it were just a regular trip to the bathroom.

Early in my career, my roommates knew the routine and understood. I had told Kenny Hubbs when we roomed together back in 1962; other roomies I had in the early days like pitcher Jimmie Schaffernoth, Dick Ellsworth and Cuno Barragan knew of my condition.

In 1965, Glenn Beckert, who would become one of my closest friends, had been called up from the minor leagues, and he and I were paired together on the road. I was red hot at the plate, batting something like .320 and having a great season. Beckert, meanwhile, was struggling, something that would be rare for him in his career.

I would get up in the morning and go through my usual routine; I took the shot in the leg, drank the orange juice and headed back to bed. But on one occasion, Beckert had caught a glimpse of what I was doing. And he didn't know I was diabetic.

That day, I went three for four. Beckert had another 0-for-4. So at dinner that night, Beckert leaned over to me and started whispering. "Say, roomie, I don't care what it is. I hate needles but I want it," Beckert whispered.

"You want what?" I answered, not having the vaguest idea what he was talking about.

"Listen, roomie, I happened to be awake this morning and saw you giving yourself a shot," Beckert continued. "I hate needles, but you're hitting .320 and I'm hitting .220. Whatever it is, I want it."

I couldn't help but laugh.

"Guess I forget to tell you," I said, obviously bursting his bubble, "but I'm a diabetic. Those shots are insulin shots. Your pancreas secretes insulin, my doesn't, so I take these shots every day."

Beckert was dumbfounded. "You take what and you are a what?" he asked.

I hadn't hidden the fact from Beckert intentionally; it was just by that time, it had become so routine it didn't dawn on me to tell everyone.

At first he didn't believe my explanation; I'm sure he was still looking for that magic potion to help him make the top 10 hitters of the league. But he saw the truth on my face.

To this day, I still take my daily shots of insulin; some days, I have to take two shots. I still do everything physically that I want to do, and it hasn't affected one part of my life. This is important for people with the disease to understand. It does CHANGE your life but it doesn't have to AFFECT the way you live it.

We have come a long way in our understanding of this disease; a long way from the days in Seattle when I was told there would never be a cure. But we still have a long way to go in terms of research, funding and education about diabetes. I'm hoping my experiences will continue to enlighten and inform people about the disease. And I'm hoping there will come a time when we don't need to raise any more money for research. That day, I'll know we have found a cure for juvenile diabetes.

My three children, Jeff, Linda and Ron, Jr., now all adults, do not have diabetes. At the time of my original diagnosis, there was concern that juvenile diabetes was hereditary. Through my studying about the disease, I had discovered reports indicating it would skip every other generation. However, now experts believe onset adult diabetes is more likely to be carried on from one generation to the other than juvenile diabetes.

I went through my family roots to discover whether there were any diabetics in previous generations. I wasn't able to dig back too far to my family ancestors in Italy or Sweden, and I wasn't able to find any traces. That has led me to believe more in the theory that a traumatic experience—such as my father leaving us at a very young age—can bring upon symptoms of the disease or the disease itself.

I have been blessed with three wonderful children.

Ron, Jr., had the burden of carrying my name in a town where everyone knew who I was and what I had accomplished. Ron played Little League in Chicago and one time when he was seven, he came to me and said he was quitting because everyone expected him to be as good as I was.

I always wanted my sons to do whatever they wanted to do and I wasn't going to be like many Little League parents and force feed them the sport. I told my son if he wanted to quit, fine, he wouldn't get an objection from me. He did stay with it, but the pressures of being Ron Santo's son continued. I wasn't aware of this when he was growing up; I didn't realize it until he was ready to graduate high school.

Ron, Jr., is a very warm, sensitive person. He had gone to his high school baseball coach and asked if he could use a different name on the back of his baseball uniform, other than Santo. He wasn't rejecting his family or his father; it was an unfair burden to put on a teenager whose father was in the glare of the spotlight every day. Many children forced into this situation might tend to rebel; he didn't. He has gone on to do some work with a landscaping company and with sports memorabilia.

Unlike Ron, Jr., Jeff didn't have the burden of carrying his father's name. He was more outgoing than Ron, Jr., and a solid baseball player. He played two seasons at Miami of Ohio as a third baseman and second baseman. Jeff had the drive to become a professional baseball player and would constantly ask me to assess his chances of making it in the big leagues.

That was difficult for me; a parent's view is quite a bit different than a scout's would be. He was looking for me to make the decision whether he should commit fully toward that goal; I wanted him to be the one to make that decision.

Jeff did make the decision himself, realizing he wasn't quite on that level that was necessary to get into the big leagues. But his second love was to write and direct, and he wrote a play, *The 25th Man*, that was produced at the Halsted

Theater in Chicago. Naturally, it was a story about the last man on the Cubs, a character named Spence Taylor, who had one good year, was earning $1 million, got vertigo, and was forced to leave the game. The play focuses on his comeback attempt and the trials and tribulations he faces.

When I saw the play, I was impressed and touched. Impressed with my son's ability to write and produce a play in a major city like Chicago; touched with the fond memories he had growing up as a ballplayer's son.

Linda, my youngest, is Daddy's little girl. I think a professional athlete looks toward having a boy, but I can say that I was very fortunate to have a little girl. Linda was born in 1969 which certainly made that the most memorable and cherished event of that year for me. Unlike Ron, Jr., and Jeff, she really didn't get much of a chance to see her dad play in the big leagues. But she became a huge Cub fan nonetheless; she plays 12-inch softball and follows the progress of her team, the Cubs, religiously. She was very excited when I got my job in broadcasting. She graduated from Loyola of Chicago in communications and wants to get into broadcast sales. She interned at a rival station of mine, and I am confident she will succeed in whatever she chooses to do in her life.

I might add I am equally proud of my stepdaughter, Kelly Reed, who I helped raise with Vicki and who is currently attending the University of San Diego, majoring in psychology.

I'm so lucky to have this wonderful family, and I'm grateful that no one in this generation of Santos has the disease that has been such a big part of my life. It's my greatest dream that in our lifetime we will at last have a cure.

fifteen

The Art of Hitting

Anyone who has ever had a bat in his hand knows that special feeling you get when you have made solid contact with a baseball; there is nothing else like it in sports—whether it's on the sandlots or at Wrigley Field.

I was fortunate. I knew that I had a God-given talent to hit a baseball. To me, the vast majority of major league baseball players today have that ability. It isn't something that can be found at a later age with physical development or constant practice. Either you have it—or you don't.

Stop and think about it. The odds are staggering. Consider how many youngsters, both boys and girls, start out at age seven or so like I did, with dreams of becoming major league baseball players. Then consider how many actually are able to take that talent, nurture it, avoid serious injury, sidestep the pitfalls of climbing up through the minor leagues and actually make it in the majors.

Then filter in the number of players who have that traditional "cup of coffee" in the big leagues and disappear into the far reaches of the small agate section of the Baseball Encyclopedia and...well...you see what I mean. Being a successful hitter in the big leagues is a one-in-a-million shot.

Hitting a baseball isn't easy. It isn't easy when you start out in the Little Leagues; it sure isn't easy when you face Bob Gibson or Roger Clemens. Still, there are great hitters out there capable of great accomplishments. I think the best pure hitter in the game today is Barry Bonds, now the 43-million-dollar man with the San Francisco Giants. He has the best mechanics and techniques; he can hit for power and spray the ball to any field. He can hit southpaws with the same ability as a right-hander. He isn't afraid to choke up on the bat but still can knock it out of any ballpark.

I was lucky. Sure, you have to make the most of it if you are to succeed, but I was blessed. I know that.

I loved baseball. I played it seven, eight hours a day on some days. I ate, drank, slept the sport. It wasn't because my mother was pressing me to do it to succeed; I honestly loved the game.

I guess I knew that I had the gift when I was seven and was the youngest player on my Little League team. All of the players on the team were older than I was, but I knew I was the best on the club. They knew it, too.

I see parents now at Little League games and I shudder. I hate to see the parents pressing their children into trying to become something they are not or don't want to be.

I wish all the parents would go simply to watch their children play and leave them alone. Let the coach of the team BE the coach. Don't become one of those overbearing parents. You can't force a kid to do what parents often demand. Now, I understand that parents want to be proud of their youngsters, but don't overdo it. Let the child learn on his or her own to love the game.

When my sons, Jeff and Ron, Jr., played, I went to as many games as I could. But I didn't put pressure on them to succeed. I wanted them to enjoy the game I loved and play it for the game's sake. If they asked a question about hitting, I would be there to offer advice. But I didn't force my views on hitting or baseball.

One thing parents have to understand is fear. Fear is definitely a factor, specifically the fear of getting hit by a baseball. We all have had it in some part of our lives on the diamond, and it is a real one. Eventually, the talented hitters get over it. If they don't, they don't ever make it to higher levels of competition in the sport. Basically, you have to put fear out of your mind. Hitting is such a mental process. Fear can only disturb your thinking and sidetrack you along the way.

Our Little League club, "The Italian Club," won the championship the first year I was on the team back in Seattle. We had to play another team that had a big, strong kid who was their pitcher. Now in most little leagues, most of the players are the same age and size. Often the biggest kid is the pitcher because he is the one that can throw the hardest.

The kid we faced in the title game was enough to make you afraid of being hit by a ball. He probably didn't look big to the adults watching, but to a seven-year-old and his eight-year-old teammates, he looked like Wilt Chamberlain.

To compensate for the fear, many youngsters put their foot in the bucket—that is, arrange their stance where they believe they are protecting themselves from getting hit. If this is done, they are doomed. No successful player can be a great hitter if he is standing away from the pitch in the batter's box. Bailing out is instinctive, and all the talks from a coach or parent won't alleviate the concern. It has to come from within the youngster himself. The mom and dad aren't at the plate.

Their child is. If he or she can't overcome the fear, a parent or a coach isn't going to change anything.

Fortunately, I didn't have to overcome much fear at the plate throughout my early years. I also didn't have to make many major adjustments as I progressed through high school into professional baseball. Major league players just didn't talk about it openly. You couldn't.

I also had good tutors along the way, but no one along the line really tried to change my style before I signed that first professional contract back in the late 1950s.

Once I did sign with the Cubs, the only person who tried to advise me about changing my hitting style was Rogers Hornsby, the Rajah, one of the greatest hitters in the history of the game.

I met him at my first instructional camp with the Cubs. Hornsby, a former .400 hitter and one of the early inductees into the Hall of Fame, suggested I stand deeper in the batter's box. I never was comfortable standing in the front of the batter's box like some hitters do and I tried his suggestion. It must have worked.

His thinking was that by standing deeper in the box, I'd have additional time to see the curve ball. Hornsby realized that I had a natural swing and didn't want to mess with it. Sometimes the most minor adjustment can make all of the difference in the world in hitting.

Some things don't change. Most of your good hitters today have a chopping swing, just like they did back then. One of the keys to this is keeping your hands away from your body. A lot of young kids believe they can attain a level swing by dropping their elbow down and in effect, swinging under the ball.

Your good hitters all swing from the top; they use their top hand as the power hand and the bottom hand as the tool to move the bat. It's like chopping wood; you must swing down on the ball. So many young players want to have the uppercut swing and wind up failing to make contact. They get discouraged and rightfully so; it's going to be more difficult to make regular contact that way.

Too many youngsters believe you have to be a big, burly guy to hit the ball into the stratosphere. They believe a big swing translates into big results.

That isn't the case. Major league baseball is filled with players who are diminutive but who pack a powerful punch. Jimmy Wynn, the "toy cannon" who starred for the Astros, and Joe Morgan, the Hall of Fame second baseman, weren't big guys but they used their arms and wrists to become great power hitters.

Even players who don't hit much for power but are good contact hitters don't need to be Jose Canseco's size. Freddie Patek played a long time in the big leagues for Kansas City and was only 5'4".

You also don't have to be an Adonis. Babe Ruth is considered one of, if not the, greatest hitter ever to put on a uniform. And everyone knows about his girth and his passion for eating and drinking. Yet he managed to have great bat speed and a level swing. And 714 times he took it out of the ballpark. Henry Aaron, who in my opinion was one of the greatest athletes ever to play in the majors, wasn't an overpowering physical presence. Yet he hit 755 home runs because of his great wrists, concentration and bat speed.

The important element is having quick hands so you can have quick bat speed. To me, that is the essence of hitting. It isn't how hard you swing but how fast you move the bat to make contact with the pitch.

We didn't do much weight training during my era like they do today. Our exercise regimen involved more isometrics than today's players that do off- and in-season weight training. But lifting weights won't make you a good hitter. I know in a lot of sports, including baseball, today's athletes believe that bulking up can translate into success. They think by building up their chest muscles they will become better hitters. But too much bulking up in the chest will slow your bat speed down. It can actually work against you.

Again, so much of this raw ability is simply a gift. That doesn't mean that every player who made it to the big leagues was gifted. I saw many solid hitters make compensation for the lack of some physical skills. Shortstop Dick Groat, who played on World Series champions in Pittsburgh and St. Louis, didn't have great power. But he adapted. He learned to hit to the opposite field and had a great career thanks to that adjustment in his stance and approach. Groat, a college all-American basketball player, was also a good enough athlete to know his own weaknesses and strengths.

Another great thing about hitting in baseball is that no two people take the identical approach because no two people have the same stance. Some prefer an open stance, others a closed one. Some players like to crouch down like Pete Rose or Ron Carew; others prefer to stand more upright like I did.

I have told countless groups of young players not to try to emulate their favorite baseball player when they adopt a hitting stance. For one thing, it's going to be very unlikely your body will be able to be comfortable in some older player's stance. The key is being *comfortable*. If you are trying to copy some stance of your hero and you feel uneasy at the plate, you are not going to be able to hit the ball. Be yourself.

When Billy Williams and I first came up with the Chicago Cubs, veteran Cubs' hitting instructor Lew Fonseca would take countless hours of films on various players and their hitting styles. This was before the advent of videotape and VCRs in the major leagues. Fonseca would sit us down and make us watch the various styles of some of the top hitters. He would slow down the film projector with each hitter to emphasize one point: they were all making contact with the ball the same way. Level swings, good bat speed and getting the head of the bat in front of the plate. It didn't make any difference whether you hit out of a coiled swing like Stan Musial or more wide apart like Willie Mays. The key was where you hit the ball.

All good hitters have patience. It is one of the most difficult things in the world to do in baseball, waiting to swing the bat and make contact. Again, it comes back to having the built-in knowledge and instinct to know to not jump on a pitcher's fastball.

Each hitter also has his own hitting "mechanism." Some players, like the Cubs' Ryne Sandberg, like to wave the bat around in the batter's box before they go into their swing.

During my career, I had the habit of wiggling my butt around before I swung. I wasn't showing off my posterior, it was just my way of getting comfortable in the batter's box.

Ted Williams, one of the greatest hitters of all time and a real student of hitting, used to say he could actually see himself make contact with the bat on the ball. He must have had great eyes. I never had that luxury.

There are times when you've made great contact and you know you hit a home run. I'm sure you have heard hundreds of interviews from players on a hot streak who say the baseball actually looks like a big grapefruit or marshmallow coming toward them. All you have to do is swing and make contact and hit it somewhere where it can't be caught. When you are on a hot hitting streak and you are staying back, the ball appears to have stopped in mid-air on the way to the plate. It looks that easy to hit. Even if the pitcher is throwing it 95 miles per hour, you are seeing it great and making contact.

However, when you aren't going well, the ball can shrink to the size of a pea. Even if the mechanics are good—you're staying back, swinging level and waiting on the pitch—you either don't make contact or you bounce it weakly back to the pitcher.

Like hitting, pitching doesn't require the arm of Christy

Mathewson or John Smoltz. Just because you're able to throw the ball at nearly 100 miles per hour does not guarantee success. The key is how you conceal what you are going to throw and whether you are able to change speeds. What made pitchers like Don Drysdale, Bob Gibson and Tom Seaver so successful and so difficult to hit is how they changed speeds. They had different velocities on their fastballs and great location. It was so difficult to see what they were throwing with their motions—it seemed the ball was coming out of their shirtsleeves.

I always found it easier to hit a guy throwing 95 miles per hour who threw from the top than someone who threw 85 miles per hour but had a different pattern of delivery and motion.

By the time you reach the big leagues, you can handle the fastball most of the time if that is all you are going to face. That's why pitchers in the game today like Greg Maddux, the former Cub ace now with that great Atlanta Braves' pitching staff, can succeed. Maddux doesn't have the greatest fastball in the league but he mixes up his pitches and his delivery so much that it's very difficult to hit him. He isn't a big physical specimen but he is a great athlete with solid pitching smarts.

Hitters are able to succeed by having a sense of what they are going to face. If they know that all they are going to see is one fastball after another, they can make the adjustment and usually cream the ball. If they don't know what is coming, if the pitcher is able to mix speeds and disguise where the pitch is coming from, the hitter is going to be in some trouble.

Control is another important factor. Pitchers who constantly are pitching from behind in the count are dead meat for good hitters. Jim Maloney threw a couple of no hitters in the major leagues and had great stuff. But he was constantly pitching from behind in the count; when he got behind he would let up just to try to get it over the plate. When a pitcher is 3-1, the batter can guess that a fastball is coming. In those situations, the batter has all of the cards on his side.

So much of good hitting is anticipation—trying to anticipate the tendencies of the guy on the mound. I'm not talking about guessing; "guess hitters" play a risky game at the plate. Some can succeed. Joe Adcock, the former slugging first baseman of the Braves, was as good a guess hitter as I ever saw, but that is probably the exception rather than the rule. If you go up guessing that, say, the pitcher is going to throw you a curve ball, and he *does* throw you the curve ball, you might knock it into a different area code. But if you guess wrong and he throws you a fastball, you're dead.

What I learned to do—and what a majority of good hitters do in the major leagues—is anticipate that the pitcher is going to throw a fastball. Anticipating the fastball allows you to stay back on the pitch. Then if the curve ball comes instead, you still have time to adjust. You won't be lunging and your stride won't be awkward.

On the other hand, if you anticipate the curve ball, you are going to wait too long. Next time you are at a game and see a guy miss the ball by a foot, chances are he was guessing that a curve ball was coming.

Naturally, this comes with time and experience. That's why rookies with great talent can have some difficulty when they first come into the leagues. They don't know the pitchers and don't know what to expect. Once or twice around the league and they are able to make the adjustments and their natural ability takes over.

This might also explain why veterans who switch leagues have some difficulty at first hitting the ball. The National League fan who is thrilled when his team acquires some monster .300 hitter from the American League can't help but be disappointed when the guy is suddenly hitting .243. But this player is suddenly facing about 130 pitchers he's never seen before. He needs time to adjust and learn the tendencies of those pitchers.

Learning about the tendencies of pitchers has its extremes. Andre Dawson of the Boston Red Sox, who had so many great years with the Cubs and with the Montreal Expos before that, used to keep a little black book, filled with notes he made about new pitchers he had faced during a season.

Other players keep charts; some managers have tapped into computer technology to analyze pitchers' tendencies. But I don't know whether all of that is necessary. During my major league career, I didn't have computers—I had my head. I stored all kinds of information in my memory; when I faced a particular pitcher, I would tap into my brain and try to hit instinctively on what I figured I would see.

I was blessed with a good memory; I would remember what a pitcher had thrown to me in a certain situation. I would remember what a guy would throw me if he was behind in the count; I would remember what a guy would throw me with men on first and second; I would remember what a guy would throw me with the bases empty. I don't claim to be smarter than anyone else who did it a different way; but I was able to hit over 20 homers 11 times in my career and over .300 four times due in part to that memory.

That is part of why baseball is so great and why it is such a difficult game to play. Some say the hardest thing to do in all of sports is hit a baseball and hit it on a consistent basis—to put a round bat on a round ball and make it go where you want it to go. They may be right.

What about the concept that you need a big, powerful bat to be a big, powerful home-run hitter? That's a myth, believe me. In many ways, the opposite is true. Throughout my career, I used a 32-ounce bat, which was about the average weight most players used in those days. Some would use a heavier bat; Richie Allen used as heavy as a 40-ounce bat on occasion.

I felt a lighter bat allowed me to have better bat speed,

better contact. Billy Williams and Ernie Banks both used 32-ounce bats and had Hall of Fame success.

I strongly recommend the lighter bats to youngsters learning the game. Forget trying to pick up that big piece of lumber. Having a lot of wood in your hands doesn't guarantee you will drive the ball farther. In fact, it's more likely that you won't have the bat speed you need to become a solid hitter.

I would always order a half dozen S-2, thin handle 32-ounce bats for the start of the season. I would also order the same S-2 in a 31-ounce size. Why? Because as the season wore on, say about late July or early August, I felt a little weaker than earlier in the year. The lighter bat felt better and gave me the same bat speed.

That's common throughout the major leagues now. Batters will go with a lighter bat as the season goes into the dog days of August. The lighter bat will give you more confidence; if a pitcher knows you can handle that inside fastball (and you will be able to do that with a lighter bat) you are putting it clearly in the mind of the hurler you have the ability to handle his best stuff. You don't have to be a big guy to use the lighter bat.

When I played in the Little Leagues and in high school, there was no such animal as an aluminum bat like there is today. I never used one during my career although I've since used them when I play in Randy Hundley's Fantasy Camps in Arizona. I understand the need for aluminum bats in many high schools; the cost of constantly replacing wooden bats puts such a strain on an athletic department's budget that it makes economic sense to go with the aluminum variety.

But that does cause a serious problem for those who want to make it to professional ball where that bat is outlawed and is likely to remain outlawed. The transition from aluminum to wood is a difficult one. With a wooden bat, you are going to likely have it broken if you are busted inside; that won't happen with an aluminum bat. The ball will jump off the aluminum bat in that situation, and it won't when you get into professional ball.

A guy who can hit 30 homers in college ball with an aluminum bat is likely to barely get 20 homers in the major leagues. Of course, if you hit 30 homers in college ball you will have developed the confidence that you can hit anywhere and that might ease the transition somewhat.

I'm dead set against the introduction of aluminum bats in the major leagues; I think aluminum bats would give the hitter too much of an advantage in the game today. Worse yet, it would distort the game and distort the records. What has made baseball unique in American society today is the fascination with records and statistics. With the advent of aluminum bats, it's likely that batting averages and home run stats would increase significantly; would you have to put an asterisk beside every new record that was established with an aluminum bat? Baseball has always taken care not to make radical changes that might distort the game. Aluminum bats would be a radical insertion.

Sure, the game has had its share of minor changes: the height of the mound, the distances to the outfield walls in the new parks, expansion, domes. Artificial turf.

Artificial turf came into the game early in my career. It changed the game by putting greater importance on a runner's speed and the speed of the ball as well. I can't tell you how many times I saw Pete Rose chop down on the ball and have it bounce for a hit on the artificial surface. If he had taken the same swing in Wrigley Field on the grass, the result would have been a ground out.

Yet the game remains pretty much the same as it did when Abner Doubleday laid out the first diamond. It's still 60 feet, 6 inches from the rubber to the plate; it's still 90 feet from one base to the next. It's still three strikes and you're out. That's why baseball has stayed the national pastime for more than a century.

Here's a question for all real fans: which position requires the best athletic ability? Well, I can tell you that I definitely wouldn't vote for the pitchers. I never considered pitchers to be very good athletes, especially compared to other positions on the playing field. I faced a lot of pitchers who could do just one thing: pitch. They couldn't hit the ball, couldn't run very well or field the position. But they had good arms and were able to stay in the major leagues.

To me, great athletes who pitched in my era were those like Bob Gibson, Kenny Holtzman or Don Drysdale. Today, Greg Maddux certainly falls into that category. In addition to having great arms, they were outstanding fielders who helped themselves out and made life tough on hitters because they made the plays at their position. They were extra infielders, not just throwers. In addition, they could hit. Gibson and Drysdale were dangerous at the plate, even as the ninth hitters in the lineup. They didn't take those namby-pamby three whiffs at the ball and walk slowly to the dugout. They were out there to help drive in runs. These were good athletes who knew that hitting was a part of the game.

As an aside, that is why I don't like the designated hitter rule. It covers up for the inadequacies of a pitcher by allowing a player to hit for him four times a game. No other sport allows a player this type of "luxury." In basketball, if you get fouled, *you* take a free throw—you don't call for a pinch shooter. You may not be the greatest free throw shooter on the team, but it's your responsibility as an athlete to be ready to take those shots.

To me, it's the same way with pitching—if you know you're going to be in the line-up, be ready to go to the plate. When Ken Holtzman went over to the American League and had all that great success with the Oakland A's, I thought it was a shame he didn't get to hit and show what a great athlete he was. It was no surprise to me when he delivered a key hit for the A's that helped them win a World Series game back in the 1970s and which helped them eventually win the world's championship that year.

The other eight position players in baseball have to do it all: hit, run and field—or they don't stay in the game. Pitchers, if they throw well, can stay no matter what. A pitcher can hit like a grandma and run like a truck, but if he's powerful on the mound, all is forgiven. That's why I think that pitchers are the worst athletes on the field.

I will say this, however, to show you that I'm not blinded by my love and passion for baseball. To me, the best athletes in any professional sport are basketball players.

A good basketball player can do just about anything in any other sport. Michael Jordan of the Chicago Bulls is a good example. Jordan is a great basketball player but also is a great golfer; he can also can hit a baseball a long way. He's just a great all-around athlete.

Like so many professional athletes, I played a lot of golf, and still do. I think the reason so many pro jocks love the game is because it is quite possibly the most demanding of all sports. Professional athletes are great competitors and love to be challenged. Golf, by the very nature of the game, is the most humbling game there is. It is an impossible game to conquer. You come close one day, but the next time out it can eat you up.

I'm not willing to generalize that the baseball players of today are better athletes than in my day, but one thing is radically different. In my era, after the conclusion of a season you put the glove and bat away and didn't pick it up again until right before spring training five months later. Today, ballplayers may take a month or so off before they're back in the indoor hitting cages or down in Florida or Arizona working again.

To me, though, it is important to get away from the game. So much of the game is mental, and your mind needs the time off as much as your body does. With a 162-game schedule, it is important to shut it down for a while. If you don't, you're going to be mentally worn down by the end of the year unless you are one of those two teams that makes it all the way to the World Series.

Today's players stay in shape all season and off-season long. They report to camp in shape. True, some players in my day wouldn't take as good a care of their bodies as they should and would report to camp overweight. I never had that problem; I was active all winter playing racquetball or basketball so my weight wouldn't be a concern when it was time to report.

When I went into spring training, I had two primary goals. One was to get in playing shape, baseball shape. Second, I wanted to get my timing. I believed it was essential to hit at least .300 in spring training, .400 if I could. I know it is fashionable for people to claim now that spring training statistics are meaningless. If you had a poor spring at the plate no one would remember come September. But to me, getting my timing and eye back was essential. By the time we were at the end of the spring training schedule and we were playing the full nine innings, I wanted to be hitting like I would at mid-season. If I had a good spring, I would be entering the regular season with a good mental attitude.

It didn't always work that way. In 1966, I was off to a slow start in the spring and hit only .209 in mid-June. But then I caught fire and wound up hitting .312, one point off my career high.

Batting practice in the spring and the regular season was my classroom. I did my homework in the batting cage so I would be ready for the exams when the games would begin. I had a set routine. I would get to the ballpark virtually the same time every game. I would take my infield practice virtually the same way every game.

In the batting cage, there was no fooling around like you sometimes see if you get to the ballpark early enough. I would get loose and take some swings without taking any stride. I would hit to the opposite field to begin my routine and then try to pull about 10 or so pitches to left field. Then I would get out of the cage and wait my second turn. In that next go-round, I would try to drive the ball as I got more loose and more relaxed. At the end, I would take as many balls as I could out of the ballpark. I was then ready for the game.

I know some players who follow similar routines. Others will get in there and work on their bunting or hitting to the opposite field. Others will try to pull as many balls out of the ballpark. I think that is dead wrong. The key is to get into the cage and work on keeping your routine.

When I would have a slump, which fortunately was rare, I would often just stay away from the cage altogether. Sometimes I would take extra BP, depending upon what I thought I needed.

We had coaches that were there to help if we needed it. But I found my best batting coach was Billy Williams. I'd like to think I helped him out the same way. Billy and I would often talk for hours about our mechanics and the pitchers we were facing. If one of us was in a slump, we'd offer suggestions on how to make an adjustment. We had an old saying, "The shorter the stride, the quicker the bat." There is a huge temptation when you get into a slump to become over anxious, a mortal enemy of good hitting. When you get antsy, there is a tendency to move your body ahead and that will force you to drag your hands behind you.

Another way to get out of a slump is to view what you're doing when you're red-hot; it is surprising how often you can pick up a minor flaw when you view yourself slamming the ball all over the park.

Billy and I worked well together from Class AA ball on. He hit in front of me and would watch me when he would get on base. We shared similar hitting philosophies. This was no knock on any of the hitting instructors we had during my tenure with the Cubs. I just respected Billy's opinion more than anyone else's. It's no coincidence that Billy has become one of the premier hitting instructors in the game today and why he has been in that capacity for the better part of his non-playing career.

To be honest, there may not be much a hitting coach can do for a veteran who has played 10 or more years in the league. A hitting instructor is more valuable for young players who are just breaking into the big leagues.

I suppose there is an element of immortality in the mind of a professional athlete—he wants to believe that he will be able to do what he does forever. You can't tell a 22-year-old that someday he won't find that hole in the offensive line, or that he won't be able to skate past the opposition for a 50-foot slap shot.

I'm sure I didn't foresee the day when the skills I had developed throughout my athletic career would begin to disappear. I do know this: It wasn't a physical deterioration that led to my retirement. If anything, it was mental.

I started realizing a problem in 1973 in my last year with the Cubs. We had a game against the Cincinnati Reds late in the season, and I had injured my thumb and was forced to use what they called a U-1 bat with a thicker handle and no knob. It was more of a singles' hitters' bat, not what I was used to.

In this particular game, I took a fastball down the middle. Johnny Bench, who by then had become a close personal friend, remarked to me as he threw the ball back to the pitcher that I didn't normally take that kind of pitch.

When he said that, I reflected for a moment and knew he was probably right. I knew there was the possibility the end was near. One year later, I hung it up.

All players go through this realization during their careers; the smart ones hang it up; the others stay on too long.

The big salaries of today's players may change part of

that. I just don't see the player of the 1990s staying around and having a long career like I did. The economic incentive for a long career isn't there—today's players can make so much money faster. It would be different if there were only the one-year contracts. But too often with multi-year contracts you see performance taper off. Look it up; hitters who ink those big, long-term deals usually slip in the ensuing year or years after the contract. As a result, I think many of the existing career hitting records will last longer than you may think. I don't think we'll see anyone get more than 4,100 hits or 755 home runs. The players with the potential to do those things probably won't stay in the game long enough to reach these milestones.

It may carry over to single season hitting records as well. It has been more than a half century since someone has hit .400 in the major leagues, and I don't think it will happen again. Heck, a .300 hitter is becoming more of a rarity these days. There is a simple explanation. When I broke in, pitching was 50 percent of the game. If you could knock the starting pitcher out, chances are you would go on and win the game and score a lot of runs.

Today, pitching is at least 85 percent of the game. You knock a starting pitcher out, and in comes some relief pitcher with just as good—if not better—stuff. The era of specialization is at hand in the major leagues and that weighs to the advantage of the pitcher. When I broke in, the starter usually stayed in deep into the game, even if he was getting his brains beaten out. Complete games are a rarity today, and it's not unusual for a hitter to face a different, fresh pitcher two or three times in a game.

Equipment has also changed to the benefit of the defense; five-finger gloves that looked more like mittens made it easier to have hitters get balls through the infield in the "old days." Today's gloves are bigger and better. Those balls don't always get through any more.

Toss in the travel demands of playing in 13 different cities in either league and you can understand why I think a hitting renaissance isn't likely to take place. I don't think the evolution of hitting in baseball has slowed; I just believe the dawn of the stopper has made doing what Ted Williams or Rogers Hornsby did nearly impossible.

sixteen

Competitors

I have had the privilege of playing in what many consider to be the golden age of baseball, those great years of the '60s and '70s. A glance at the number of Hall-of-Famers I faced would give much credence to that assumption.

The Dodgers' Don Drysdale was as tough a competitor as you would ever want to meet. He was an intimidating sort, not the kind of pitcher you find these days around major league baseball. He thrived on pitching inside. Now, I'm not talking about brushing you back occasionally, I mean he threw at you. His philosophy was that the plate was his, and you as a batter were in his space. He threw three quarters, meaning that ball would be coming in at you at around 90 or 95 miles per hour. He wanted you off the plate, period. He wanted to establish the outside part of the plate in the umpires' minds.

I never disputed this type of competitive spirit. He didn't do it to upset you.

Over time, Drysdale and I became friends. But when I first broke in and the Dodgers were developing that great staff of Drysdale, Sandy Koufax, Johnny Podres, et al., he would pitch me like he'd pitch the others: tight. If I didn't get out of the way, it was my neck.

So I figured after we became friends he'd stop throwing me. Oh, sure. He pitched me the same way, chin music, whenever possible.

When I was in high school, I was watching him pitch on TV. My mother was there, too.

"Mom, I don't know how I'm going to ever hit a guy like Don Drysdale. He's so big and throws so hard," I said. "I might never be able to do this. God must have given him something special."

Just after I said that to my mother, Henry Aaron stepped to the plate and hit a monster home run off Drysdale.

"Mom," I said, "the Lord must have given Aaron a little more than he gave Drysdale."

Two years later I was facing Drysdale and the Dodgers at Wrigley Field on the national game of the week.

First time up, I walked. "I used to watch this guy on TV, and he looked tough," I said to Ernie.

"You have to look at every pitcher in the big leagues as if they were Class AA pitchers," said Banks. "Don't look at them as Drysdale or Koufax. They should be minor league pitchers in your mind."

Great advice, poor results. I'm sure all my pals in Seattle were watching the game on TV when I went 0 for 4 in my first of what would be many encounters with Drysdale.

After the game, I went back home and called my mother, something I would do on a regular basis throughout my career. "Did you watch the game, Mom?" I asked.

"Remember two years ago in the living room I told you how tough Drysdale would be to face? I can tell you now he's even tougher when you actually face him."

You didn't mess with this man. If you were able to get a hit the first time, you could count on an inside pitch that would knock you off your feet. He did it to me. I understood.

Today's game is different. The batter believes the plate is his and any pitcher that throws near you should be ready to get charged from the batter's box. Pitchers are afraid to throw inside. The good ones, Roger Clemens, David Cone, Doc Gooden, Greg Maddux, will throw it inside. But a majority of them are afraid to.

Bob Gibson threw hard, too, probably harder than Drysdale. Gibson wasn't afraid to put you on your ass. But he used his reputation to perfection; he got a lot of guys with fastballs on the outside part of the plate.

But Gibson was as mean as Drysdale. The difference between the two was that you could guarantee an inside pitch from Drysdale; Gibson threw harder all over the plate. And Gibson might have had as good if not better stuff. He was known as a fastball pitcher but he had a tremendous hook—a great curve that would fall off the table.

It was a great era of pitchers in the '60s. Drysdale, Gibson, Juan Marichal, Fergie, Steve Carlton, Tom Seaver, Koufax. I'm often asked to compare eras; how would these guys do now against some of the best? Sure, I'm biased, but these guys could get anyone out, then and now.

Now, Seaver, he had surprising stuff. He wasn't afraid to challenge you even though he didn't pitch inside as much as a Drysdale or a Gibson. On one particular key night in New York in 1969—a mid-season game at Shea Stadium, before the infamous September showdown—Seaver was on top of his game. He zipped through our lineup the first two times out with relative ease.

That second time around for me was a classic

showdown. He got two strikes on me, and I kept fouling off one pitch after another. Might have been six or seven foul balls. I kept waiting for him to make a mistake, he kept waiting for me to take one too close to the corner. He later said it was one of the best at-bats anyone has ever had against him. Unfortunately—he got me out.

So we went into the ninth inning. The fans knew Seaver had a perfect game with two out in the ninth, and I'm sure most of the guys on our bench knew we were going in the history books as Seaver's first no-hitter/perfect game victim. Worse yet, it would be the first no hitter in the history of the Mets franchise.

Leo sent Jimmy Qualls to the plate as the sacrificial lamb—the guy in the trivia question about who got the last out in a perfect game. Qualls was a journeyman ballplayer who like some, just seemed to be able to come off the bench cold. Well, cold or hot, we knew this game was over.

And then unbelievably, Seaver made a mistake. He threw a fastball down the middle and Qualls laced it to center. The perfecto was imperfecto. And to this day, no Met has ever thrown a no-hitter.

We weren't so lucky four years earlier against Sandy Koufax. We were out on the Coast in 1965 at Dodger Stadium and we were scheduled to face Koufax. We had Bob Handley going. It didn't take Jimmy the Greek to figure out the odds on us winning that night weren't great. Koufax was at the top of his game, the best pitcher in baseball on a team that would go on to win the National League pennant that year.

Koufax was one of the rarities in the game; he never had bad stuff. When he first came up, he was a hard throwing southpaw with little control. But he learned through the great Dodger system how to paint the corners. He had learned not to throw his best stuff in the first inning. He would build into that great 95-mile-per-hour fastball. By the seventh inning, he was actually throwing HARDER than in the first inning. You don't see that in today's hard throwers. When you faced Koufax, you geared for the great fastball. He eventually developed a "drop" ball, the same location as his fastball but it broke straight down. It was murder.

That night, Bob Kennedy called a meeting before the game to go over the Dodgers and Koufax. Actually, it was kind of silly. What are you going to learn about Koufax in a meeting?

Al Spangler, our centerfielder at the time, got up in front of the locker room. "Not to worry fellas, I've got all of Koufax's pitches," said Spangler, who had played with Koufax and the Dodgers for a couple of seasons before coming over to our ballclub. "I've got their signs, too. I've got their tendencies. I know when Sandy is going to throw that curve or fastball in the stretch position. When he comes down from the stretch and leaves the elbow out, it's a breaking ball. When it is closer to his body, it's a fastball."

Spangler was a great bench jockey. He could give you tips and sometimes they even paid off. On this night, I suppose we left the meeting with a little more confidence against Koufax than in the past because we had Al Spangler on our side. Once Koufax got into the stretch, he was dead meat.

Kessinger led off for us as usual, with Beckert second and Billy Williams third. I figured if we got a couple of guys on, I'd come up, take Spangler's inside information and knock this guy into the Santa Monica Harbor.

Kessinger popped up and Beckert struck out. Beckert would always tell me as I approached the on-deck circle what kind of stuff the pitcher had that evening.

After Beck fanned, I said to him, "What do you think?

"So-so," Beckert replied. Wow, I thought. So-so stuff and Spangler on our side. It's going to be a rout.

Williams popped up, end of the first.

In the second, I stepped to the plate, brimming with confidence and what I thought was inside information. First pitch, fastball. My bat didn't move. Second pitch, fastball. My bat didn't move. Now I realized Spangler's information was only helping me if we got a guy on base. We didn't have anyone on base; I was sitting there 0-2 and the bat hasn't left my shoulder.

Koufax was efficient. He didn't waste pitches trying to set you up. Maybe that is why when he pitched, the games were under two hours.

The next pitch was another fastball. All knee high. All strikes. My bat hadn't moved, and I was out.

As I made the walk back to the dugout, I looked for Beckert. "So-so stuff?" Who is he kidding? So I searched for Beckert. Couldn't find him. He was hiding at the end of the bench.

I yelled to him. "That's right, Beck, he doesn't have shit, does he?"

Twelve other times Koufax struck us out. The only hard-hit ball was by Bryan Browne, who was playing center for us that night.

Into the ninth, Koufax got our first guy out and then faced Joey Amalfitano, who would later coach and manage the Cubs before becoming a long-time Dodger third base coach under Tommy Lasorda. Amalfitano whiffed on three pitches. Harvey Kuenn, who was one of the top hitters in the American League before coming to us at the end of his career, was the 27th batter of the game for us.

Amalfitano walked to him and whispered, "It's not worth it, Harvey. You might as well not even bother to come to the plate." He went anyway, and Koufax had his no-hitter.

Ironically, our man Handley was nearly perfect on the mound. He gave up just one hit and one run. We lost 1-0. We headed into the clubhouse, a combination of awe and dejection. Needless to say, it was quiet. Our guy pitched great, theirs pitched better. We were overmatched.

I finally jumped up and yelled, "Time out. Where's Spangler?"

Spangler was at the other end of the locker room. He finally showed his face.

"Well, Spanky, I never saw him do this," I said, referring to Spangler's elbow theory.

Koufax's gem was the second no-hitter thrown against us that year. Jim Maloney, a pretty good right-hander with the Cincinnati Reds, also befuddled us in the first game of a doubleheader at Wrigley Field. He was all over the place that afternoon and walked 10 but did not give up a run.

Eventually, they scored a run in the 10th, and we lost the game 1-0. Maloney always had no-hit stuff. He didn't get the same kind of rave notices that Koufax or Seaver would get but he was one outstanding right-hander.

During my career, I played in six no-hit games, four for us and two against us (the two by Maloney and Koufax). For us, Kenny Holtzman threw a pair of no-hitters, including the important one in 1969 and again against the Reds in 1971. Burt Hooton threw one in April against the Phillies the following year, and Milt Pappas came within one batter of a perfect game and settled for a no-hitter in 1972 against the San Diego Padres.

In the Pappas game, he had retired 26 straight batters and was facing pinch-hitter Larry Stahl. He had a 3-2 count on him and threw him what looked to me like a knee high strike for what should have been the third out and the completion of the first perfect game in Chicago Cubs' history. Instead, umpire Bruce Froemming, someone I eventually grew to like and respect, called it ball four. I just felt that Froemming missed the call. Pappas got his no-hitter but lost the perfect game.

That night on television, I saw the replay. I was surprised Stahl took the pitch; I was even more surprised that Froemming had the balls to give it four balls. Froemming continued that reputation throughout my career and is still doing it his way today.

All-time, all-star teams are great hot stove debate

topics. I'll admit my years in the WGN broadcast booth have broadened the scope of my all-time team. The perspective is a bit different from the booth than it is on the field. As a player, you aren't scouring the newspapers for other guys' batting averages or game winning hits. You pay more attention to that kind of thing as a broadcaster.

Sure, I'm biased. I'm a Cub fan. Blue blood. I root for the Cubs. I still think, however, I'm a good judge of talent. So here goes:

Ernie Banks is my all-time first baseman of the players I've seen or played against. You can't measure the mental intensity this man had along with great physical skills. Two times an MVP, back-to-back, and 500-plus home runs. Unfortunately, and I know it's been said a lot—playing in Chicago, never playing in the World Series, it just didn't give Ernie Banks the kind of national exposure he deserved. I do believe had Ernie Banks played in the '90s, he would be among the superstars of any sport. He would have been Michael Jordan.

People forget that when Ernie and I played, the exposure of the team nationally wasn't the same as it is now. There was no cable TV, no superstation. There were a lot of newspaper guys covering us then because there were more newspapers, but the reach of the game wasn't the same as it is today. Accomplishments in the '50s and '60s might have exceeded those of today, but they weren't replayed over and over again on ESPN or CNN.

You also have to remember the transition Ernie Banks made. He started as a shortstop and was outstanding. He was no Ozzie Smith but for a big man, he made the plays. He made the transition to first toward the end of his career. Let me tell you something about first base. Too often, we have the concept that whoever is the worst fielder we stick at first. We're ingrained with that concept from Little League right up to the majors. Well, in Ernie's case, that was incredibly wrong.

Ernie was a good fielding first baseman; he was as good a first baseman as he was a shortstop. One of the reasons our infield in the 1960s was so good was because Ernie could dig out any throw that came his way. In that way, he's a lot like Mark Grace is with the Cubs today. Grace finally received the credit he deserved in 1992 when he won his first Gold Glove. Believe me, a good first baseman like Banks or Grace can save you from many errors during the course of a season and more importantly, save your pitcher from getting into a lot of needless jams.

My all-time catcher is Johnny Bench. Offensively, he's in a class by himself. Defensively I think some people underrate Bench, although in my opinion he had the best arm in the game when I was playing. What also impressed me about Bench was the way he could call a game. The Big Red Machine didn't have the kind of pitching staffs that say, the Atlanta Braves have today. They didn't have four or five guys who could go out and give you nine innings every start. True, Sparky Anderson handled their bullpen with great talent, but a lot of the credit should go to Bench.

Second base, no debate. Ryne Sandberg is the best now, maybe the best ever. Kenny Hubbs could have fallen into that category had his life not been snuffed out. Hubbs was Sandberg's equal defensively. But I doubt whether Kenny could have put up Sandberg's numbers at the plate.

Much is made about Ryno playing at Wrigley Field and that might inflate his offensive numbers. That's ridiculous. He has some detractors, and I've heard the complaints. But go ask a general manager if he wouldn't want Ryne Sandberg as his second baseman right now. Even in his 30s. A lot was made about Sandberg getting that $7 million deal in early 1992. I don't believe that anyone in the game deserves $7 million a year. But, and it's a big but, if I were forced to have to pay someone $7 million, Ryne Sandberg would be the man.

My shortstop is Ozzie Smith. Maybe because I'm

partial to guys who can field the position, the Wizard is the best. He also plays on artificial turf. He's got the great range, he's acrobatic, slick. Makes all the plays. Our guy, Shawon Dunston, has quite a cannon at short, too, maybe one of the best arms I've ever seen. But Ozzie Smith, especially considering how long he has excelled at the position, is the best.

Third base? Eddie Mathews of the Braves.

Surprised I didn't say Santo? Hey, I was fortunate to play at a time of great third basemen in baseball. I patterned myself after Don Hoak who used to play for the Pirates. Hoak played third the way it should be played; aggressively. He dove over everything. Kenny Boyer of the Cardinals was another great one. Naturally, I didn't see much of Baltimore's Brooks Robinson who broke in shortly before I did. Robinson was probably considered the greatest fielding third baseman in history—no one gets that many Gold Gloves by accident.

But Mathews was clearly the best I'd ever seen. From recent years, you'd probably have to consider Mike Schmidt of the Phillies. Right now, there aren't a lot of great third basemen. Matt Williams of the Giants and Chris Sabo of the Reds are probably one-two in my book, even though Terry Pendleton has had great back-to-back seasons to lead the Braves.

My all-star outfield may be easier. Hank Aaron, Willie Mays and Roberto Clemente if I can't count my own teammate, Billy Williams. If it was a golden age of baseball, it certainly was a a golden age of baseball for outfielders. I really don't think until another generation passes that we will really appreciate the greatness of these three players.

Mays was fun to play against, even though he'd find ways to beat us all the time. I played 13 years against Willie Mays and he may have the best skills of anyone I ever saw. He did everything well. Today, a guy gets $4 million if he can hit or $4 million if he is a great defensive player. Willie Mays was the best all-around athlete I ever saw. He could hit, hit with power, run and throw. Excelled at everything.

Aaron may actually have been a bit underrated. Underrated? People talk now about Aaron and it's the 755 home runs. Truly a great feat. That's 40 homers a year for about 18 seasons. But Aaron was an excellent base runner. He would steal a base on us and would go from first to third with the best of them.

Clemente was flashier than Aaron. He was the best defensive outfielder I ever saw. Andre Dawson has about as good an arm as anyone now, and he's about as close to Clemente as you can come. Clemente could have gotten more accolades now from people outside of Pittsburgh if he, like Hubbs, hadn't died in an airplane crash.

As for today's players, there is tremendous talent out there, but there are certainly some players I would take a pass on if I owned my own club. I wouldn't want Jose Canseco on my team. Tremendous talent, tremendous headache. I'd rather have a guy like a Lenny Dykstra or John Kruk, now both with the Phillies, than Canseco. Dykstra and Kruk constantly bust their butt for you. They don't have Canseco's skills but they don't have Canseco's attitude problems, either.

I always had respect for the hard-playing hustler— that's how I played the game and that's how I expected others to play. Before Pete Rose made it fashionable to run out balls, dive head first into the bag or get his uniform dirty, I was doing it. I wasn't the only one; it was just the way we played back then.

Let me say outright, I believe Pete belongs in the Hall of Fame for his accomplishments. You don't get 4,100-plus hits and not belong in Cooperstown. In the same breath, though, he did damage to the game. There are reasons that baseball bans gambling.

Honestly, baseball is a hard game to fix or alter. About the only way you could ever consider even trying it, I suppose, would be to get to the pitcher. And even if someone throws it right down the middle of the plate, it doesn't guarantee someone is going to be able to hit it or hit it where it couldn't be caught. That's the stuff of Hollywood movies, not reality.

Yet, the hint of gambling stains for ever. Did Pete hurt himself? Yes. Did he hurt baseball? Yes. But he still belongs in the Hall for what he did as a player. I admired Pete Rose because of his philosophy about baseball. I was sad to see him go down with the gambling allegations and be banned from baseball. Rose didn't have the same God-given talent as say, a Johnny Bench; Rose made the most of out of his abilities. He had worked so hard at the game of baseball and for this to happen to him was a tragedy.

As for the subject of cheating, if any Chicago Cub or an opponent I faced corked the bat, I wasn't aware of it. Even if they did, you still have to hit the ball on the sweet spot on the bat. Pitchers were another story. For example, everyone knew that Gaylord Perry was doing something funny to the ball; I never complained to anyone about it. If I did, I was falling victim to the mind games that Perry wanted to play. He had more of a psychological effect on hitters making them guess whether he was loading up the ball than he actually did by throwing a spitter.

Today it's more difficult to determine whether something illegal is being done by the pitcher due mostly to the advent of the fork ball. It behaves the same way as a spitter or a cut ball, and that's possibly why you see so many hitters asking the umpires to inspect the ball.

As far as the best manager I ever played against, I'd put two in that category. Gene Mauch, the fiery skipper of the Phillies and Expos, and Sparky Anderson, who had the great years with the Big Red Machine.

Mauch knew the game of baseball and could get the best out of the talent he had. He wasn't afraid to try new things; he was an innovator. One game against the Phils at

Wrigley Field, I was at the plate in the bottom of the ninth with the game tied and one out and the bases loaded. Mauch brings one of the outfielders into the infield, giving them five infielders. Four of the infielders were on the left side of the infield, meaning they were playing me to pull. They had two outfielders, one in center and one in left. NO ONE IN RIGHT FIELD.

I'm a career pull hitter and I'm not thinking of going to right. So, I top the ball, dribble it down the third base line. The third baseman lets it go, hoping it would go foul. Instead, it hits the bag and we win. It was great, innovative strategy, the kind Mauch was famous for; unfortunately for him, it just went our way.

Anderson also knew the game inside and out. He handled the pitching staff to perfection and more importantly, he was always one step ahead of the action. Both he and Mauch weren't afraid to yell encouragement from the dugout.

I'm glad I was considered a fiery player. I think umpires understood my philosophy on the game and as a result, I didn't have a lot of trouble with most of them. I wasn't thrown out of that many games; I never kept a count. I do know I wasn't thrown out of any game in the early innings. I believed I was more valuable to my team in the lineup than in the clubhouse.

Today, when you see a guy get tossed in the first three or four innings, chances are that's a selfish player who has his own agenda. If a player gets tossed early like that, he's hurting his team. Don't buy the argument the player just lost his temper. Most umpires give you a little leeway, not a lot. But if you show them up, even early, they're going to toss you.

The only umpires I really had a problem with were the lazy ones, the ones that didn't hustle or make the effort to make the call. I didn't make a huge stink if the umpire hustled and was in a position but still called it wrong.

Jocko Conlan, one of the most colorful and competent

umpires in the history of the game, was the type of umpire you could talk with all of the time. He was one of the best if not the best umpire I ever saw.

He would start jabbering with you from the moment you walked up to the plate until he might have called you out on a third strike. But Jocko was fair and more importantly, consistent. He set a high standard for the other umpires that worked with him on a particular crew and for the rest of the National League.

As for the media, I had a very good working relationship with the media in the cities we played in. I know I might have been spoiled in Chicago for the great broadcasters we had while I was a player.

It was easy to like Jack Brickhouse. He had the reputation of being a homer, a guy like me who loved the Cubs. But Jack never shied away from his tag. He never tried to pretend to be something he wasn't.

I'll tell you something else about Brickhouse. Jack was as good an interviewer as I ever encountered in my career. He would get more information out of you from a five minute session than anyone else in journalism. It's easy to dismiss him as a big Cub fan who did our games, but he also knew how to get to the heart of a story.

Jack would also do something that is rare today; he would always ask the right questions to make whomever he was interviewing look good. How many people can say that about themselves?

Brickhouse is in the Hall of Fame. He belongs there, just as Harry Caray does.

Harry is quite different than Brickhouse. It is easy for fans across the country to think of him now as strictly a Cubs fan or for singing, "Take Me Out to the Ballgame" during the seventh inning stretch. But when I played, Harry Caray was the biggest St. Louis Cardinal fan you would ever want to meet. He would root for them with the same zeal he has now for the Cubs. But that never bothered me or a majority of the players. He was a great salesman for baseball. Anyone who has given more than 45 years to the game like he has, well, you take your cap off to him.

Like Brickhouse, Harry is a great interviewer, something that is also overlooked because of all of the flash and glitter associated with his style. He absolutely, positively, knows baseball. He never played the game but he understands the nuances of baseball.

Journalism is different today than it was when I played. When I played, newspapers ruled the roost; there would be four guys from four newspapers regularly going to our games; New York had more because they had more newspapers. I don't know how much reporters knew then of the insides of what was going on privately with the players; if they knew, they didn't write about it.

Today, there are no secrets from reporters. Everyone's life is an open book. Something that is done on the field or said after a game is beamed across CNN or ESPN within hours of the game. If it helps promote baseball, I'm for it. I do believe there is a line to be drawn regarding the private lives of athletes regardless of the number of media out there hungry for a story.

Things change, and then they change again. Lights in Wrigley Field? Who would have thought? It has long been suggested that one of the reasons we lost in 1969 and never won a pennant was the fact Wrigley Field didn't have lights. You know how this one goes; we were stuck out in the hot sun wilting while other teams got to play their home games at night. Well, I've never bought that one. Day baseball didn't contribute to any lack of success we might have had in the standings.

When the Tribune Company bought the club in 1981, I heard that they would immediately put in lights. So when the decision came five years later to go ahead and install lights, I wasn't surprised or disappointed. But I also understood that without lights, there would be no more Wrigley Field. I firmly believed the Tribune Company would build a new stadium elsewhere because it wasn't economically sound to continue to play 81 day games. I was more in favor of keeping Wrigley Field than ensuring that the institution of day baseball would live forever.

Anyone who has ever played or seen a game in Wrigley Field understands the special nature of the park. In today's era of cold, cement cereal bowl stadiums, Wrigley Field stands out as the best place to watch a game. Day or night.

The sight lines are excellent; you are right on top of the action. On the field, you CAN hear what the people are saying in the stands. In the stands, you can see the ball curve from the pitcher's mound. The ballpark has character: the ivy on the walls, the scoreboard that still puts up the scores inning by inning; the intimate atmosphere that is lacking in so many other ballparks.

I'm glad there is a trend back to the Wrigley Field-like structures like Camden Yards in Baltimore and the new field to be completed in Cleveland.

Second to Wrigley I always thought Dodger Stadium in Chavez Ravine was the best ballpark I ever saw. It had a lot of atmosphere and in many ways was like Wrigley Field. No ivy but the setting is tremendous. And it is immaculate. The fans are great; they get a bad rap for supposedly wanting to all leave in the seventh inning to beat the traffic. But these are great baseball fans.

If you were tired from the long trip out to the West Coast, stepping onto the field to take batting practice at Dodger Stadium got your juices flowing again. Sure, the great Dodger teams may have helped in that regard, too.

While Dodger Stadium was near the top of the list, Shea Stadium in New York was at the bottom. You can tell there is little about New York or the Mets that I care for.

Shea Stadium just doesn't seem to be like a major league park; the constant roar of the planes make it seem more like you're playing at the end of the runway.

I got to play in basically two eras: the end of one with the old parks like Crosley Field in Cincinnati with its incline in the outfield; Forbes Field in Pittsburgh where I broke in to the majors; the old Busch Stadium in St. Louis with its right field pavillion; for a brief time, Connie Mack Stadium in Philadelphia; the old Polo Grounds in New York that was home to the Mets before they headed out to Flushing. These were great ballparks; this was the way baseball was meant to be played.

About halfway through my career, those parks all seemed to disappear overnight. Riverfront Stadium, Three Rivers Stadium, Busch Memorial Stadium and Veterans Stadium in Philadelphia all were built within a three- or four-year span. We went from the great parks with the natural turf to the new-look fields that had Astroturf. There were times you didn't even know what city you were in playing in.

That is what makes Wrigley Field special; it's a part of Chicago. You know looking at the OUTSIDE of Wrigley Field where you are and that you are a part of history; I don't think you can say that about most of the other parks in the game today.

Now as an announcer, I still get goose bumps walking up through the stands to the press box, hearing the fans scream, " Hi, Ron!" or even "What about 1969, Ron?"

It's baseball the way it should be played; I hope they never tear it down. I hope they keep refurbishing and renovating Wrigley Field forever. I'll know wherever I am that I played third base for 14 seasons there, for the love of the game and for the love of ivy.

Index

For more information on juvenile diabetes,
write to the Juvenile Diabetes Foundation:

JDF Chicago Chapter
70 West Hubbard Street
Chicago, Illinois 60610

JDF International Chapter
432 Park Avenue South
New York, New York 10016

FOR THE RECORD

RONALD EDWARD SANTO

Born February 25, 1940, at Seattle, Washington
Height 6'0", Weight 194 lbs.
Threw and batted righthanded.

Established major league records for most years leading league, assists, third baseman (7), 1968 and most consecutive years leading league, assists, third baseman (7), 1968 (both since broken by Brooks Robinson, 8); most years leading league in chances accepted (excluding errors) (9), 1969.

Tied following major league record: Most years leading league, double plays, third baseman (6), 1971.

Established following National League records: Most assists, season, third baseman (393), 1967 (since broken by Mike Schmidt (404 in 1974); most games played, third base, 162-game season (164), 1965; most double plays by third baseman, career, 389, 1973; most chances accepted, lifetime, third baseman, 6462, 1973; most assists, lifetime, third baseman, 4532, 1968; most years leading league in games (7), 1969.

Named third baseman on THE SPORTING NEWS NATIONAL LEAGUE ALL-STAR TEAM, 1966-67-68-69-72.

Named third baseman on THE SPORTING NEWS NATIONAL LEAGUE ALL-STAR FIELDING TEAM, 1964-65-66-67-68.

Year Club	League	Pos.	G.	AB.	R.	H.	2B.	3B.	HR.	RBI.	B.A.	PO.	A.	E.	F.A.
1959—San Antonio ....Tex.		3B	136	505	82	165	35	3	11	87	.327	158	246	53	.884
1960—Houston.................A. A.		3B	71	272	40	73	16	1	7	32	.268	72	148	16	.932
1960—Chicago ....Nat.		3B	95	347	44	87	24	2	9	44	.251	78	144	13	.945
1961—Chicago ....Nat.		3B	154	578	84	164	32	6	23	83	.284	157	307	31	.937
1962—Chicago ....Nat.		3B-SS	162	604	44	137	20	4	17	83	.227	167	343	24	.955
1963—Chicago ....Nat.		3B	162	630	79	187	29	6	25	99	.297	136	374	26	.951
1964—Chicago ....Nat.		3B	161	592	94	185	33	13	30	114	.313	156	367	20	.963
1965—Chicago ....Nat.		3B	164	608	88	173	30	4	33	101	.285	155	373	24	.957
1966—Chicago ....Nat.		3B-SS	155	561	93	175	21	8	30	94	.312	157	408	26	.956
1967—Chicago ....Nat.		3B	161	586	107	176	23	4	31	98	.300	187	393	26	.957
1968—Chicago ....Nat.		3B	162	577	86	142	17	3	26	98	.246	130	378	15	.971
1969—Chicago ....Nat.		3B	160	575	97	166	18	4	29	123	.289	144	334	27	.947
1970—Chicago ....Nat.		3B-OF	154	555	83	148	30	4	26	114	.267	144	320	27	.945
1971—Chicago ....Nat.		3B-OF	154	555	77	148	22	1	21	88	.267	128	275	18	.957
1972—Chicago ....Nat.		3-2-O-S	133	464	68	140	25	5	17	74	.302	119	282	22	.948
1973—Chicago (a) ....Nat.		3B	149	536	65	143	29	2	20	77	.267	107	271	20	.950
1974—Chicago ....Am.		2-3-1-S	117	375	29	83	12	1	5	41	.221	135	148	8	.973
National League Totals.....................			2126	7768	1109	2171	353	66	337	1290	.279	1965	4569	319	.953
American League Totals...................			117	375	29	83	12	1	5	41	.221	135	148	8	.973
Major League Totals			2243	8143	1138	2254	365	67	342	1331	.277	2100	4717	327	.954

(a) Traded to Chicago White Sox for pitchers Ken Frailing and Steve Stone, catcher Steve Swisher (plus pitcher Jim Kremmel), December 11, 1973.